Why We Left Mormonism

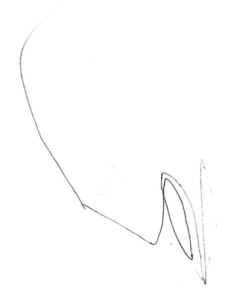

Why We Left Mormonism

Eight People
Tell Their Stories

Latayne C. Scott

BAKER BOOK HOUSE
Grand Rapids, Michigan

Copyright 1990 by
Baker Book House Company

Formerly published under the title
Ex-Mormons: Why We Left

ISBN: 0-8010-8306-0

Third printing, April 1992

Printed in the United States of America

Scripture quotations in this volume are from the King James Version of
the Bible. Chapter 8 "Latayne Scott" is excerpted from *The Mormon Mirage*
(Zondervan, 1979), 1988 edition. Used by permission.

To seven courageous people: Cindy, Kevin, Sheila, Thelma, Sandra, Randy, and Dave; as well as the valiant Christians who brought them to Christ.

To Kathy Champney, whose encouragement and transcription skills made this project manageable.

And to my Lord, whose sacrifice for me has made my every forfeiture seem small in comparison, and whose reward of himself has been abundant compensation.

Contents

Introduction

When Kin Millen, an acquisitions editor for Baker Book House, contacted me almost two years ago to suggest that I write another book about Mormonism, I had a ready answer, one I had given many times before to similar suggestions.

"I wrote everything I know about Mormonism in *The Mormon Mirage*," I laughingly told him.

But it was true—I had done research for almost two years to write *The Mormon Mirage*. I had combined that with my ten years' experience as a faithful Mormon, and the painfully produced product has stayed in print, with one small hiatus, for ten years. I had even revised the book twice, making minor changes and because of the grace of God the timing of these changes kept me from falling into the Mark Hoffman forged-document trap. (In the 1980s Hoffman forged several crucial documents purporting to relate to Mormon history and doctrine. These forgeries have cast doubts on the veracity of genuine documents and have ever since complicated research of both Mormons and non-Mormons.) Overcoming such obstacles, the information in *The Mormon Mirage* has been reliable and generally up-to-date for readers during that decade.

I was not interested in writing *The Son of the Mormon Mirage*. But Kin, in that gentle way he has, explained that he didn't have in mind another book about Mormon doctrine, but a book specifically about people who have left the Mormon church—and their reasons for doing so.

That idea intrigued me, because it reflected the two questions that I am most often asked when people talk to me about my experiences in leaving the Mormon church.

The first question that I am invariably asked is, "What was the one thing that 'put you over the edge' in your decision to leave the Mormon church?" People are always interested in that phenomenon—that "point of departure" or particular circumstance in which a person breaks free of a system of thinking and makes a major change.

The second question is a heartbreaking one, a plea that comes in different forms, asked in different voices, by different people all over the country whenever I speak about Mormonism. I can see replicated over and over in my memory the sight of eyes, some reddened, some pleading, searching my own for answers. The question takes this form: "How can I convince my loved one [husband, wife, son, daughter, mother, father, friend, fiancée] that Mormonism is wrong?"

I could be a millionaire if the answer to that question could be sold, for I have no doubt that many of the people who ask it would not only sell all they have, but mortgage all they would ever hope to have, to gain assurance that what they could tell that loved one would cause him or her to see the falseness of Mormonism. But as Simon the magician learned to his dismay, the power of the kingdom of God is never for sale: and its commerce is from heart to heart.

That is what I wanted this book to be—a communication from heart to heart.

When I first began to make lists of people I believed would be effective in answering those same two questions I am always asked, I marveled at how the Lord had prepared me to meet so many who would qualify. I remembered a trip to California, soon after *The Mormon Mirage* was published, where I met Sheila Garrigus and Cindy

Bauer and Chuck and Dolly Sackett and Michael Marquardt. A few months later I was in Salt Lake City and made the acquaintances of Jerald and Sandra Tanner. As the years progressed I met Ed Decker and Richard Baer and Bob Witte and Granny Geer, as well as lesser-known ex-Mormons (with equally fascinating conversion experiences) like Dave Wilkins and Randy Steele and Kevin Bond. Some of these I met through personal contact, some through the fellowship of praying for them as they made their tortuous way out of Mormonism. Looking back, I am amazed at how efficient the Lord has been in bringing people into my life who have contributed in so many ways to the eventual product of this book.

When I began to contact people for participation in this project, I realized that there were many more potential participants than could possibly tell their stories in one book. The first requirement I set was that I had to either know the participant personally, or he or she must be highly recommended by someone whom I know personally.

Why was that? I believe that many people have the ability to speak or write persuasively and yet when you meet them, they have a "spirit" about them that makes them ineffective for one reason or another. In other words, I didn't just want people who could spin a good story, but people who have lived valiantly as Christians in every sense of the word.

I asked some hard questions of the people I selected. For instance, I asked them to decline my invitation to be a part of this book if they had been Christians for less than three years or were not active in a local congregation. That is because many, many people leave Mormonism without ever again making a commitment to another church, and countless others drift in a spiritual limbo between Mormonism and Christianity, not fully accepting or rejecting either one. Maturity and stability have an unmistakable authority of their own, and readers of this book will recognize it in the people who are within these pages.

I sent a list of questions to the participants, along with

blank tapes for their responses. I discovered a great diversity in their experiences, as well as some significant common elements. Their stories and advice reflect not only their backgrounds, but also their very different personalities. I soon recognized that some were very fervent and animated, while others were more reserved, and that this was more a reflection of upbringing and personality than it was a barometer of love for the Lord.

I am acutely aware of the fact that all Mormons as well as many Christians will read this book with an eye critical to the validity of the salvation experiences of each person whose story is herein chronicled. There are questions that logically arise: Is escaping Mormonism tantamount to being saved? Are all ex-Mormons who join a church Christians?

To help with these questions, and to preserve the integrity of each person's story as it was told to me, I have tried to use the exact wording of each person's own choice in telling about the points at which he or she decided to leave Mormonism and at which he or she made a decision for the Lord—whether referred to as "accepting Jesus as Savior" or "giving one's life to Jesus" or any other phrase.

I know that this still leaves some unanswered questions in the minds of some readers, and for that I apologize, but such questions are beyond the purpose and scope of this book.

Some points, though, have become clearer as this book developed. It has become obvious to me that ex-Mormons are much less "territorial" than the average churchgoer, mainly because we see how much Christian churches have in common rather than what separates us. For instance, I can go into any "mainstream" Christian church in this nation and be assured that they also believe as I do that there is only one God, that his Son Jesus atoned completely for our sins on the cross, and that the Holy Spirit can indwell believers (none of which Mormons believe).

I thought it would be a little artificial to write about myself in the third person, so I have chronicled my own experiences in the first person, excerpting it from the opening chapter of *The Mormon Mirage,* and have answered the questions about witnessing in the same question-and-answer format as the other participants.

A note about the use of the term *Christian* in this book: While Mormons will argue vigorously that they are Christians, I use that term to refer to those who believe in the orthodox faith of historical Christianity, which admits to only one God, with whom Jesus was co-existent and co-equal from eternity.

Because many terms that are used in this book might be unfamiliar to most Christians, a Glossary of such terms has been included at the end of this book.

It is my prayer that the readers will feel the closeness that I feel to the other participants of this book. The most fascinating personality, however, does not have a section in this book. He has his own Book, the Bible, and what we ex-Mormons have chronicled is no more than a sidelight.

It is *his* story, in the pages of our lives, that we want to tell.

PART ONE

Personal Testimonies

There is a deliberateness about this man, Randy Steele—an orderly and methodical way of speaking. Though he is middle-aged, he is old and wise (perhaps, he might say, older but wiser) in the way he relates his decision to leave the Mormon church, but youthful in the courage of this act that caused him to give up not only his respected position as a bishop, but cost him the unity of his family: a wife and four children who are still Mormons.

1

Randy Steele

Randy Steele was born in 1944 in Springfield, Ohio. He was raised in the Methodist faith, and stayed somewhat active until high school. Then a boyish crush on a girl in Bible Club rekindled his interest, and he attended church and Youth for Christ rallies on a regular basis, though he admits he never developed a personal relationship with the Lord.

After high school, he lost interest in spiritual matters and began smoking, drinking, and became involved in other worldly activities. He married, and he and his wife Becky attended the Methodist church at first faithfully but later sporadically, without any real commitment.

During the Christmas season of 1971, two young men knocked at the Steeles' door, identifying themselves as elders in the Church of Jesus Christ of Latter-day Saints. Being the holiday season, it seemed to the Steeles a good time to learn something more about Jesus. Randy and his wife were impressed with their neat appearance in that hippie era, and invited them in. The missionaries gave them a *Book of Mormon*, told them about Christ's visit to the Americas, and set up an appointment for a lesson.

Randy was impressed with their polished presentations, their confident grasp of their material, and their easy answers to all the questions that he and his wife posed. The missionaries set a date—February 12, 1972—and challenged the Steeles to make a decision about the truthfulness of their message by that time.

As the date neared, Randy was ambivalent, but Becky was decisive. She announced her intention to be baptized on that date. To both of them, it seemed significant that her mother and Randy's father had just developed an interest in genealogy and were actively researching both family lines.

Randy prayed to receive the "burning in the bosom" promised by the *Book of Mormon* he had been reading at the missionaries' urging, but when that sensation didn't materialize, he decided that the absence of any negative feelings was for him a witness of the Spirit; and he, too, was baptized that day.

Randy was ordained to the Aaronic Priesthood shortly after his baptism. When he completed his bachelor's and master's degrees in metallurgy from the Ohio State University, he and his wife (after several moves) settled in Lima, Ohio. But just before they left Columbus, Randy was ordained to the Melchizedek Priesthood.

"My wife and I were very contented as Mormons," Randy recalls. "We enjoyed the fellowship and the energy and sincerity of our Mormon friends." Randy was a good Mormon, and held many positions and offices in the church. He worked on social committees, and held various teaching positions. He was a secretary for his Elders' Quorum, and later a counselor in that organization. Then he became executive secretary to the bishop, and later a counselor in the bishopric.

In 1981 he became a bishop, a position of great integrity

and trust in the Mormon church. In late 1983 he helped break ground for a new building for the ward over which he presided.

Randy recalls that he looked with sympathy upon non-Mormons that he knew, believing that he simply had something better. His one encounter with someone leaving Mormonism occurred when a young member of his ward, whom Randy had never met, came to his house to request that her name be removed from church records. "Apparently she had become a Christian," Randy recalls, "but she didn't bear a strong testimony to me of that; she just wanted her name removed."

Now, years later, Randy has some idea of the turmoil that caused her distress, for he is now separated, mainly because of his testimony as a Christian, from his wife and his childen, the eldest of whom recently completed a mission for the Mormon church.

Point of Departure

Randy first encountered literature critical of Mormonism just a short time after he joined the church. As a graduate student at the Ohio State University, he had occasion to be in the section of the library that housed a few books on Mormonism. Most were either accounts of the trek west, or were fictional, but one in particular caught his eye. It was *No Man Knows My History* by Fawn Brodie. This book contended that Joseph Smith was not a prophet of God. "This really surprised me," Randy remembers, "because the book mentioned that the author had at one time been a member of the Mormon church."

Greatly upset, Randy carried this distressing news to Becky, and called the missionaries who had baptized them to explain.

"Trust your testimony," was the advice of the elders. They also gave Randy and his wife a two-volume book by Mormon writer Francis Kirkham, and also a rebuttal to the Brodie book titled, *No, Ma'am, That's Not History* (Bookcraft, 1959). These satisfied the questions both Randy and Becky had, and he recalls that at later times when they bought or were given anti-Mormon books, that they just leafed through them and then put them into their library.

Randy's father-in-law, a lay minister for a fundamentalist church, had been upset from the time that he learned that Randy and his daughter had become Mormons. The months of discussion in which Randy, Becky, and he participated caused Randy, after a long time, to come to a new conclusion: Mormonism was not just another Christian sect. But he believed that Christians were deceived, and that the divisions in Christianity were the proof of this. At one point his father-in-law gave them a tape by Walter Martin. After Randy and Becky listened to it, she wrote a long rebuttal to the tape and sent it to her father. Her testimony in Mormonism, it seemed, flourished under such examination.

Randy, meanwhile, was beginning to have some persistent questions about details of Mormon history and doctrine. Little things—like why the lost 116 manuscript pages of the *Book of Mormon* were not retranslated; whether or not the Garden of Eden had really been in Missouri; why only the Mormons of all the religious factions in Missouri were attacked.

"Occasionally one of these doubts would come off the shelf of my mind where I had put it," Randy says, "and I would meditate on it for a while and then put it back. But I never, never told anyone about these doubts, because I felt it was a sign of weakness in my faith."

In the fall of 1983, while Randy was serving as bishop and working in the BP Oil Refinery, he began talking to a co-worker by the name of Mike Thaman. Mike was a Christian, and had read several books about Mormonism. In fact, he would bring whichever book he was currently reading to work, and would lay it out in plain sight by his lunchbox each day.

"It upset me, but I never said anything about it," Randy recalls. "But then one day he told me he'd like to get my opinion on one of the books he was reading, one he characterized as 'gentle.' I willingly accepted it from him because I really didn't think it would have any effect on me."

The book was an early edition of *The Mormon Mirage*, and as Randy leafed through it, he noticed the name of Dee Jay Nelson, an ex-Mormon archaeologist whose credentials were later found to be misrepresented. Randy had just recently read an exposé of this man, and felt that the rest of the book was as false as he was.

"I was really anxious to read it," Randy reminisces, "because I had never before studied an 'anti-Mormon' book in any detail all the way through." The process took several months, since Randy only read the book half an hour a day during his lunch time. The experience was a tumultuous one: "A number of things I had put on the shelf of my mind started coming down off that shelf and wouldn't go back onto it."

During this time, he mentioned nothing to his wife, nor even to Mike who had given him the book. But one day as Randy was walking between two buildings at work, he saw Mike approaching. Without thinking, he said, "I've got to talk to you about that book you gave me. I've finished reading it, and I feel there are some things in there that are truthful, things I don't think the church can refute."

Mike was sympathetic, and set up a time for them to meet together. "You don't know how much trouble that book is going to cause me," Randy said. He outlined for Mike some of his areas of concern, and Mike agreed to pray for him and to help him in any way that he could.

Randy's next move was to write to Bob Witte, whose name was listed in the back of *The Mormon Mirage* as being with an organization called Ex-Mormons for Jesus. In the letter, Randy gave Bob his office phone number and address, since no one else but Mike knew what he was contemplating.

"I kept it all to myself," Randy remembers, "for I was in a position of responsibility and leadership." He felt that he could not risk the testimonies of others on his doubts.

Bob Witte called Randy a few weeks later and shared the story of how he had come out of Mormonism, and his reasons for doing it. He also gave Randy the name of another ex-Mormon, Dick Baer, who sent Randy books and materials, in care of Mike.

Finally Randy's conflicts surfaced. He wrote a letter to his stake president asking to be released from his position as bishop. Because the stake president's job involved extensive travel, it was an uncomfortably long wait for Randy for a response.

Meanwhile, Randy's turmoil increased. He found himself unable to relate to people at church or to talk to them about spiritual matters. Most difficult of all was the prospect of sharing his findings and fears with his wife, Becky.

Another friend at the refinery, Bob Buhrow, was a Christian man who supported Randy during this stormy time. One day while visiting Bob about some refinery business in his office, Randy shared his feelings of distress and helplessness. They prayed together, and at Bob's urging, Randy asked the Lord to come into his life.

"I can't really describe the feeling I had after that," Randy recalls. "I was still pretty mixed up about the whole thing, but I knew there was something different now. I had closed part of my life behind me and was opening another part."

The new part was even stormier. When Randy decided to tell his wife one Sunday afternoon what he had been experiencing, Becky's reaction was immediate and overt. What Randy had hoped would be a private communication within their bedroom walls disintegrated into shouting and arguing. She immediately called the first counselor to the stake president who agreed to meet with them that evening.

"You never did have a testimony," was the counselor's assessment of the situation.

Then why was I called by divine revelation to be a bishop? Randy thought.

Still dissatisfied, Randy made arrangements to meet with Augusta and Dan Harting, a couple that Dick Baer had recommended. They drove the three hours from their home in Indianapolis to meet with Becky and Randy in a motel room, because Becky didn't want them in her home. Their conversation was an intense one that lasted almost four hours.

The next day Randy learned that Becky had contacted a couple, Bob and Rosemary Brown, who lived in Mesa, Arizona. The Browns had written *They Lie in Wait to Deceive*, a book which dealt with the false credentials of Dee Jay Nelson, the archaeologist mentioned earlier. Bob Brown shared some archaeological items of interest to Randy—such as the fact that there is a South American river named Moroni, and that the Nephite money system is similar to that of the ancient Egyptians—and invited Randy and Becky to come to Mesa.

The Steeles spent three days in Mesa, touring the Mesa Temple's visitor center and meeting with a number of people the Browns had contacted to come to their home. One man, who was formerly a Congregationalist minister, testified to the truthfulness of Mormonism, and another man came with a boxful of books that he used to show Randy the veracity of Mormonism.

"He had a copy of the *Matthew Henry Bible Commentary* which he claimed was a very rare book, one of the last obtainable before they went out of print," Randy recalls. "He read a passage out of it that seemed to be an appeal for something like Mormonism, saying it was necessary." (Randy later learned that the Matthew Henry commentaries are still in print; in fact, they are available at any Christian bookstore.)

All the people who the Browns presented to Randy and Becky had one message: people who teach against Mormonism are unstable, and frequently have grave moral problems in their lives, and delight in making a profit at the expense of Mormons.

Rosemary Brown had her own explanation of why

Randy had been "targeted" by so many people critical of the Mormon church. After intently poring over his genealogy, she announced that one of Randy's ancestors was related to Joseph Smith. "This is why they are after you," she said, "because you are related to the Prophet."

Though Randy had been warned by the Hartings about the pressure that the Browns and others would put on him to stay in the Mormon church, he had no idea it would be so intensive, so persuasive. He began to feel himself wavering. His original intention was to allow Becky to see the tactics they would use, and now these same tactics were affecting him! She became stronger and stronger, while Randy could only say, "I'm not sure what I believe."

"I knew you'd see the light," Bob soothed, his arm around Randy. Toward the end of their visit, Bob arranged that their return plane flight take them through Salt Lake City. A friend of Bob's set up appointments for Randy with Roy Doxey and Joseph Wirthlin, both men prominent in the Mormon hierarchy. These two men assured Randy of the truthfulness of the Mormon gospel, and the visit concluded with Wirthlin giving Randy a special priesthood blessing.

When Randy returned to Ohio, he went through a seesaw series of events. First of all, he learned that there had been a concerted effort by several Christians at his plant to pray for him. Randy was too embarrassed to tell Mike and the others about his confusion over the weekend's events, so he asked Mike to make sure that no one talked to him about religion at all for a while.

Frequent calls from the Browns in Arizona gave him a lot to think about. They told him about a couple, the Coes, who had left Mormonism and told their story in the film *The Godmakers*, but who had rejoined the church. Randy was eager to meet them and ask them about this decision. (Much later, however, he learned that they again left Mormonism.)

Some of the books about Mormonism that Randy had ordered and had had sent to Mike's house arrived, but

Randy refused to read them. Mike, however, did read them, and a little at a time would share short passages from some of the books, primarily from the Tanners' book *Mormonism: Shadow or Reality?*

"These little bits of information would surprise me," Randy remembers. "I was totally unaware that such things had happened in Mormonism, though Mike assured me that they were documented in such a way as to be beyond question."

Randy's brother-in-law, a Christian with whom he had shared his decision to accept Christ, came for a visit to Lima. He, Randy, and Becky spent an entire evening discussing Christianity and Mormonism.

"I pretty well nailed him on several points, don't you think?" Becky asked after her brother-in-law departed.

"Well," Randy admitted, "there were a lot of things he said that made sense to me."

When Becky pressed Randy for the reasons for such feelings, it soon came out in the conversation that Randy had been discussing Mormonism with his friend Mike at work. She arranged a meeting with Mike in which she insisted that Mike not talk any more to Randy about Mormonism.

About this time two apostles of the Mormon church came to the area to select a new stake president. Randy, like other ward and stake leaders, was granted a private interview. Even though Randy was not concerned about being called to the position of stake president, he had his interview with the two apostles. He told them about his problem, and they assured him that they knew of his struggle, and gave him a special priesthood blessing.

"I felt like I was walking on cloud nine," remembers Randy, "I had been given a blessing by two apostles of the Lord Jesus Christ. But even with that, the doubts kept coming back, stronger and stronger."

At work, Mike had done his best to honor Becky's wishes and did not bring things to Randy's attention as he had before. But Randy could not contain the questions that constantly plagued him, so he would ask Mike questions, mainly about Christian doctrines that differed greatly from those of Mormonism.

Though Randy's wife had told only a few people about Randy's ongoing inner wrestling, many people in his ward began to notice signs of it. He was finally released from his position as bishop, and as more of his friends became aware of the cause of this action, some of them suggested a Bible study. To this Randy readily agreed, with the provision that the Christian point of view be represented by Mike and his wife and a pastor they knew who had experience in defending Christianity.

"It was a stormy study," Randy recalls. "There was a lot of debate over items in the Bible, and the pastor, who was well versed in the Bible, defended it well. The Mormons attempted to attack it, but with little success." The study finally sank under the weight of scheduling problems and the fact that there could be no compromising on such opposing positions.

The Sunday after the last Bible study, in November, 1985, Randy finally stopped attending the Mormon church, and went to Mike's church, and there made public his testimony of the Lord Jesus Christ. Shortly thereafter he was summoned to appear before the Stake High Council, which he did in April, 1986.

"My heart was beating so hard that it could be heard across the room," Randy ruefully admits. This was literally true—because he actually had two heart valves that were particularly noisy that emotional evening. But he had prepared a written list of his reasons for his loss of faith, a copy for each person present and had written on the reverse side his testimony of the Lord Jesus Christ. The court decided not to excommunicate him, though they did honor his request to remove his name from the church rolls.

He and his wife are now separated.

Dave Wilkins is an active, fervent-speaking man whose warmth permeates the story of how he, as a young adult, left the Mormon church which he and his ancestors had so long advocated.

2

Dave Wilkins

Dave was born in Blackfoot, Idaho, in 1941. Blackfoot at that time was composed of the town proper as well as little rural communities that surrounded it, and Dave recalls that he only knew of four or five families in that entire area who were not members of the Mormon church. Each little community had its own Mormon chapel, rivaling softball teams, and a way of life that made a little LDS boy growing up at that time believe that Mormonism was the only way of life imaginable.

Both of Dave's parents were Mormons and came from a long line of ancestors who were also church members. It has ever been a point of family pride that his mother's great-grandfather was Wilford Woodruff, who was the prophet of the Mormon church at the end of the last century. Dave's mother has been actively involved in the Mormon church her entire life, in spite of Dave's father's lack of corresponding enthusiasm. But he and his own father (Dave's paternal grandfather) were like many Mormon men who, though not active in church, nonetheless would never have dreamed of leaving the church which was their social, cultural, and family epicenter.

One family, however, who lived across the road from the Wilkins, had left the Mormon church and attended an Assembly of God in a neighboring town. Though they were regarded somewhat as outcasts in their own community, Dave recalls that this didn't seem to matter much to them—they were good neighbors, friendly in spite of the standoffish attitudes that some had toward them. The neighbor man would make homemade kites, get them airborne, fly them for hours, and then tie them to fence posts where they would remain aloft for days in the persistent Idaho breezes, perhaps somehow symbolic of the buoyant faith of the lone Christian family in the undercurrents of Mormon community life.

Dave recalls being baptized into the Mormon church when he was eight, in the stake center in Blackfoot, along with several others who had reached that age which for Mormons is the time when children reach accountability. This is something Dave recalls vividly—even more vividly than other later experiences in the church. He advanced through the offices of the Aaronic and Melchizedek priesthoods, as did all the other boys of his age in that little community, leading prayers, passing communion, giving two-and-one-half minute talks in Sunday school, collecting fast offerings, accompanying older men on home-teaching assignments.

He and his family moved to Nevada, and after a year of college at the University of Nevada at Las Vegas, Dave joined the military. Both in boot camp as well as in training, Dave was actively involved with Mormonism, wherever he was transferred. While in Alaska, for instance, he often accompanied Mormon missionaries when they went to homes to present lessons to prospective members. He was installed in a ward position, and the church and its members were the center of his social life. When he was later transferred to Alamogordo, New Mexico, he worked with the ward youth group, and steadily dated a Mormon girl there.

The situation in this young woman's family undoubtedly had a great influence on Dave's later life, for here he first saw a family that was composed of one Mormon (her mother), a Methodist (her father), and children who attended the Mormon church with their mother. "But the mother wasn't very happy," Dave recalls, remembering the pressure put on the father and the problems that his dogged resistance caused.

Dave helped convert several people to Mormonism while he was in the military. "I was never really happy with the canned lessons and the approach the missionaries used—asking questions that would trap people into certain responses. I think I thought that the end justified the means, and if you could get these people to recognize truth, they would pick up on it later. I didn't necessarily like it, but my purpose was to convert them."

After leaving the service, Dave attended Brigham Young University in Provo, Utah, for a semester, and then took a job in the South Pacific, first as a construction worker and then later as an oiler. He returned to Brigham Young and later transferred to New Mexico State University, where he ultimately obtained a bachelor's degree in agricultural economics and a master's degree in civil engineering. There also he met LaNell, the pretty young Baptist woman who was to become his wife.

Today Dave and LaNell live in Albuquerque, New Mexico. They have two teenaged children, Lori and Glen. Dave works as a hydrologist for the United States Geological Survey. The entire family is an active and valued asset to the Montgomery Church of Christ in Albuquerque.

Point of Departure

What made Dave Wilkins go from a fourth-generation Mormon to an active member of a Christian body? A series of incidents led up to this transition. The first was the feeling, already mentioned, of discomfort with the methods used by Mormon missionaries in converting people.

Another incident occurred when Dave attended his first non-Mormon church service. Up until that time he had unconsciously accepted the fact that Mormons were different from other believers, but he had just as unconsciously assumed that everyone else was "weird," as he put it, and that Mormons were the only normal ones—religiously speaking. But after attending the only church service available to him on the remote island where he was stationed, Dave came away with a realization that perhaps others too might have something of value for him.

His first real doubts about the divine nature of the Mormon church, and specifically, its claim to direct revelation from God, occurred his first semester at BYU, when he was living in a house near campus with five other young men. A church official came to the house and asked Dave to teach a class in the university ward he attended. "I was surprised," Dave says, "because there were several returned missionaries in the house with me, and I knew that I wasn't qualified to teach, at least not nearly so qualified as any of them." Over his objections, he was cajoled into teaching the class, "and not doing a very good job," he ruefully adds. His faith in the procedure of "divine calling" to such a teaching position was shaken when it was later learned that another roommate, also named Dave, was the one who'd been "called" to that position.

But Dave's most serious breaking point of faith occurred far away from BYU—in fact, far away from almost all civilization. He was working out on a remote area named Johnston Island, "an atoll, really," about 600 miles west of Hawaii. This island was populated by several racial and cultural groups, among them Japanese, Filipinos, Hawaiians, and Caucasians; and this diversity was reflected in the Mormon church that was there, too.

One Sunday morning the serene Pacific air was racked by the sound of shouting. In the middle of the church service, some of the Hawaiians had begun to angrily accuse the Caucasians of exploiting the island's resources, saying that the Mormons were just as responsible as any others. What followed, Dave says, "was almost a donnybrook."

Seeing his brothers fighting and shouting at each other was beyond the understanding of the young man who had grown up with a strong sense of community interwoven with his faith. *We are all supposed to be Mormons,* he thought, *not fighting like this.*

But this isolated incident didn't seem isolated in Dave's mind. He began to wonder what else was under the surface, and vague feelings of something "not quite right" simmered on back burners of his mind.

He returned to Brigham Young University, and there battled with rising feelings of resentment toward a system there that favored conformity and penalized those who deviated. And Dave, now a young man in his mid-twenties who had chosen to join the military and work instead of going on a mission, felt the pressures of this system. Classroom situations, teacher preferences, housing availability, and especially dating and social life were all "tipped" in favor of the "R.M." or returned missionary.

There were others at BYU who felt the same way he did. They congregated together in nearby restaurants over cups of coffee, outcasts who increasingly distanced themselves from the "politics" they saw.

His resentment heightened when he was interviewed by a ward official. Though Dave was not ashamed of his "kind of life," he saw the whole incident as a type of invasive grilling. He questioned in his own mind the right of someone to ask personal questions of another he hardly knew.

It was in this state of mind that Dave decided to return to the mountains of New Mexico he had seen when he had been stationed there, to New Mexico State University at Las Cruces. By this time he was attending the Mormon church only sporadically. He began to withdraw from the activities of the church, "drifting away," as he says, not toward anything in particular, but certainly away from Mormonism.

It didn't really matter then to Dave that the cute young woman with the bright-blue eyes whom he saw one morn-

ing in the school cafeteria was not a Mormon. He overlooked this in her in the same way that she overlooked the
fact that he was the only man she'd ever met who wore
real Blackfoot Indian beaded moccasins on campus. And
so their romance began.

It was not until after they married that the subject of
children and their religious training became an issue.
LaNell was a Baptist, a fervent believer. They decided to
"try out" each other's church—Dave remembering the situation of his former girl friend's family—and they both
became increasingly frustrated with this course of action
that became more and more painful.

"LaNell was willing to give Mormonism a try. But we'd
go to the Mormon church and she'd come home crying,
because of what she had heard there. And I'd go to the
Baptist church and I'd come home complaining because
the preacher's oratorical style seemed like he was yelling
at me. There wasn't much middle ground."

Their four years of married life in Las Cruces saw no
relief to this situation. The Mormon home teachers would
visit, and LaNell would be upset by their references to
Mormons' becoming gods, and Dave would be put off by
the histrionics of her preacher, even though he thought he
was otherwise a pleasant person.

LaNell even took the missionary discussions in an
attempt to understand Mormonism (and her husband!)
better, but when she declined to be baptized, one of the
elders told her that Dave would be better off if he would
divorce her and find a nice Mormon girl to marry.

When they moved to Austin, Texas, both LaNell and
Dave decided that their new life there could not follow the
pattern they had set in Las Cruces. LaNell had had several
friends who were members of the Church of Christ, people
she had admired, and she remembered their reputation for
deep Bible knowledge, and so she suggested that she and
Dave attend a Church of Christ. This decision was cement-
ed when their new insurance agent suggested that they
attend his church. During the nine months they lived in

Austin, they attended a fledgling congregation that was meeting in a school cafeteria.

"Only the Bible, that's all that was taught," reminisces Dave. "I had never heard things presented like that, and LaNell was happy because it was just the Bible."

They moved then to Denver, Colorado, and the space where they parked their mobile home turned out to be next door to a couple who were members of a local Church of Christ. The Christians there were loving and kind toward Dave, LaNell, and their new baby, Lori, and when they moved six months later to Yuma, Arizona, they knew where they would attend church.

During all this time, though, Dave who had made a mental break with Mormonism, had not made any commitment to Christ and to his body, his church. He and LaNell had attended church in Yuma for about six months before one of the elders there, Larry Moore, asked Dave if he would like to have a private Bible study. Dave's first inclination was to brush off the suggestion, but since Larry's petite wife, Doris, had thrown dinner in on the bargain, they accepted.

The Wilkins stood the Moores up that first night—but with good cause: LaNell delivered their son, Glen, that evening. When the Moores deduced what had happened, they arrived at the hospital with gifts and flowers.

When they finally had that first study, it was a relaxed, hands-on look at Scriptures that had nothing to do with Mormonism, just what the Bible says about how to become a Christian. As the weeks of study progressed, Dave looked forward to this time to learn the Bible. "I began to see contradictions in what I had previously believed," Dave says, "and how Mormonism conflicted with the Bible." But it was almost three months into the study before Larry thought to ask Dave about his and LaNell's religious backgrounds. When Dave answered, "Mormon," Larry just shrugged and said, "Okay," much to Dave's relief.

About a month later, Larry asked Dave, "If it came

down to deciding between the two, would you choose the Bible or the *Book of Mormon?*" Dave answered without hesitation, "The Bible." After he and LaNell talked about it, they decided to both be baptized, and about twenty members of the congregation came to the church building that evening to witness: a show of support and love and fellowship that the young couple never forgot.

Though Dave's father referred to their decision to become members of the Church of Christ as "a compromise," Dave and LaNell never saw it as such. To them it was the end of a long search, not only for a church they could both attend, but also a search for answers to questions that both of them had felt for many years.

There aren't many people who leave Mormonism and then go on a full-time mission—for life. But the same zeal and enthusiasm that caused Cindy Bauer to live as a "super Mormon" has carried over into her new life. What might be termed in others "the Christian walk" is, for this suntanned young woman with the intense eyes and forthright manner, more a "Christian sprint."

3

Cindy Bauer

Cindy Bauer was born in 1946, in Glendale, California. She moved to Castledale, Utah, shortly thereafter, where she lived until she was in the second grade. She returned to California but continued to spend her summers in Utah, an unwitting link between these two states where the bulk of the Mormon population of the United States resides.

Deep within her heritage were Mormon ancestors who had crossed the Plains before 1865, many of them the products of early nineteenth-century missionary efforts by Mormons in England, Scotland, and Ireland. Her mother was a "Daughter of the Utah Pioneers." Her Latter-day Saint family ran the gamut from the name-only "jack Mormons," to the active non-temple-marriage members, to her uncle, who was a high priest.

Cindy's uncle baptized her when she reached the age of eight, and the memories of being lowered into the baptistry by his strong arms, the swirling of the water around her little white dress, and the impact of the words of her confirmational blessing are still fresh in her memory.

She was educated in Southern California, first in public schools and then for two years at Cerritos College. During this and subsequent years of her life, she was very active, sometimes holding as many as three church teaching jobs at a time, in every auxiliary organization of the Mormon church, except the exclusively male priesthood. She taught in the Junior Sunday School, from the little "Sunbeams" all the way up to the older children. She taught Primary, in the Mutual Improvement Association of young people, and in the women's organization, the Relief Society.

To someone with no Mormon background, these are just names and titles. But the list goes on, overwhelming just in its bulk. For two years she was an instructor in the Seminary program, teaching *Book of Mormon* and Old Testament. She also substituted in the college-age Institute program, and was the Missionary Representative on campus. In the adult Sunday School she taught Gospel Doctrine class and genealogy, serving as her ward's genealogical authority.

In the early seventies she served a lay mission for the church, at the Hill Cumorah Pageant in Palmyra, New York, which depicts the finding of the *Book of Mormon*'s golden plates there and the *Book of Mormon* story.

Why this herculean effort at teaching the doctrines of her faith? "I can remember teaching people that Joseph Smith said that if you fail to do your own genealogy, you do it at peril of your own salvation," Cindy recalls, "and I'm sure that's what motivated me there. But I considered teaching any Mormon doctrine an exciting part of my life."

She recalls that even in high school her identity as a Mormon was very high profile, as was that of many of the other school leaders and class officers. The two young men she dated during high school, as well as her best friend in college, all joined the Mormon church due to her influence.

At the age of twenty-one she made a commitment to read the *Book of Mormon* from cover to cover and then asked God to reveal its truthfulness to her. "I can remember," she says, "kneeling in prayer and looking down at my chest and seeing it literally on fire"—an explicit confirmation of the *Book of Mormon* promise to readers that they would experience a "burning in the bosom."

She lived the Word of Wisdom, the church's health law, paid her tithing, and had a "burning testimony" of her belief that Joseph Smith was a prophet of God. This testimony intensified after she traveled to Nauvoo, Illinois, and visited the jail cell where Joseph Smith died. After hearing the familiar details of his "martyrdom" given by the full-time missionary-guide there, and seeing the spot he claimed was the prophet's blood, Cindy was overcome with emotion and deep love for Joseph Smith.

The Mormon church was the focal point of her life's activities, even her thoughts. She loved the church and was deeply satisfied by every element of it. Leaving the church—either for herself or anyone else—was completely inconceivable.

She looked with amazement at "Gentiles"—non-Mormons—and though she never thought of them as a lower class of people, she saw them as "golden contacts," proto-Mormons, any one of which would certainly become a Mormon if the opportunity were provided. "Until late in my teens, I thought it was impossible for someone to have listened to the missionary lessons and not join the church." Even after experience taught her that this could not be true, she still carried the assumption that "everyone really wished they could be Mormons, but that they were not able to live the strictness, the stalwartness, the high calling of being a Mormon."

But, as Cindy learned, the greatest test of strength that would be required of her would be not in living as a Mormon, but in leaving Mormonism. Today she lives far away from Salt Lake City and its atmosphere, in beautiful Maui, Hawaii. There, she and her husband Tom and four daughters Carla, Christy, Cari, and Charis serve as full-time missionaries. Tom and Cindy have been missionaries since 1979, and with her help Tom directs the Youth with a Mission program. Together they oversee between six and

eight schools a year, training young adults for short-term
and long-term evangelism work and mercy ministries.

The Bauer family may be removed from the environs of
Utah, but their hearts are still with the Mormon people.
They have traveled extensively throughout the South
Pacific and behind the Bamboo Curtain, smuggling in
Bibles and Christian literature, especially that which deals
with Mormonism. Tom, in fact, was responsible for some
of the first translations into Chinese of tracts that show the
errors of Mormonism. Their work focuses not only on the
South Pacific and Asia, but also on Utah, "the most
unevangelized state in the union," where they are planning a YWAM headquarters in Salt Lake City.

Point of Departure

Cindy was living in Ohio in the early 1970s when she
escorted a group of young Mormon girls to the national
Dance Festival sponsored by the LDS Church. This trip
included a sightseeing tour of Salt Lake City's Temple
Square. As the group pressed their way into the gates, a
lone man stood facing them, just outside the grounds. As
Cindy passed him, he pressed a small tract into her hand.
Cindy put it in her pocket. It stayed there until several
days later when Cindy idly put her hand into her pocket
and drew out the pamphlet she had forgotten about.

Most of the material in the tract dealt with some of the
more "far-out" claims of Joseph Smith—that the Garden of
Eden was in Independence, Missouri, that the Ten Lost Tribes
were on a land mass that had been taken from the North Pole,
and some other things that might have been shocking to anyone but a "total, sold-out Mormon" like Cindy.

For years she had believed and openly taught such
things as the Mormon doctrines that God was constantly
having sexual intercourse with his celestial wives to produce spirit babies, just as Cindy believed that he had done
to create her own spirit body. She believed that he had had
such intercourse with the young girl Mary to produce the

body of Jesus. She had taught this and other doctrines, too—such as the Mormon doctrine that when one is baptized into the Mormon church that one receives an actual transfusion of new blood, making him or her a member of one of the twelve tribes of Israel.

So this tract didn't shock her. The only thing she hadn't seen before was a bizarre teaching, attributed to Joseph Smith, about a site in Mexico being the location of the City of Enoch. Cindy remarked to herself with satisfaction that she had "another exciting thing to teach that Joseph Smith had said."

Then she turned the tract over. There, on the back, was Cindy's first view of the simple plan of salvation—one that did not include those "essentials" such as temple worship or priesthood or even a strictly organized church—a plan that emphasized Jesus Christ and his dying for the sins of each person.

That experience lay like a dormant seed in her heart for four long years, years in which she forgot its message and turned her full powers toward the Mormon gospel that she believed would ultimately make her a goddess.

The first rays of God's light, the first sprinklings of the water of his Word, fell on that seed in 1975 when Cindy was working in Bellflower, California, at a Mormon-owned firm. Her boss was also her bishop, later a first counselor to the stake president. His wife was Cindy's best friend; and almost all her co-workers were Mormons, many of whom were active or returned missionaries, seventies, and held other church offices.

Cindy would have thought that there would be a contrast between these Mormons and the non-Mormons who worked there, and she was right. But one Christian co-worker stood out in a way she didn't expect. Not only did he live as exemplary a life as any of the Mormon men there, he outstripped them in every area of integrity and openness. Every Mormon there considered it his or her personal responsibility to get this fellow to join the Mormon church, where they felt he belonged.

This young man would listen carefully and courteously to the Mormons who taught him, but would always find opportunities to talk to them about how much he loved his Lord, and how simple the plan of salvation the Bible taught was. He introduced her to Christian friends with morals and ideals she thought existed only within Mormonism, and invited Cindy to Spirit-filled church worship services that had a powerful impact on her.

He knew Mormon doctrine well too. Most of the things he would tell Cindy that might have shocked a less-entrenched Mormon did not bother her at all. But he continued, persistently, trying to find chinks in her Mormon armor.

His first effective strike occurred when he called Cindy on the phone with a simple question—a technique that seemed to disarm her and challenge her to action. "Does the *Book of Mormon* teach the fullness of the gospel?" he asked.

Cindy had just finished teaching the *Book of Mormon* in seminary the previous year. "Certainly!" she replied, echoing what the seminary manual had emphasized, and what the *Book of Mormon* insistently claimed for itself.

But Cindy was in for a shock when she began looking for material from Mormon sources that would support her assertion. The *Doctrine and Covenants* claimed that the "fulness of the everlasting gospel" was in the *Book of Mormon*, so Cindy went to the authoritative source, *Mormon Doctrine* by Bruce R. McConkie, for clarification. She was shaken when she read the definition of "gospel" found there. "The gospel of Jesus Christ is the plan of salvation," it read. "It embraces all of the laws, principles, doctrines, rites, ordinances, acts, powers, authorities, and keys necessary to save and exalt men in the highest heaven hereafter."

Cindy was stunned by the realization that the *Book of Mormon* contains almost *none* of the teachings that Mormons say are necessary for salvation in the celestial kingdom: temple rites or garments, priesthood offices such as seventy and high priest, eternal progression, degrees of glory, or baptism for the dead. Feelings of helplessness and disbelief shook her.

Another time she was sitting in a class discussion where someone casually mentioned the fact that the Mormon

Church had changed its official name three times since its inception—at one time it was simply known as the Church of Latter-day Saints. "I had harped for years about how the name of the church showed that we were indeed Christians," Cindy says, "and then I found out Jesus was at one time not even in the name. I wondered, *Couldn't Jesus make up his mind on the name he wanted for his church?*"

A growing group of concerned Christians began to witness to Cindy of the power of Jesus in their lives. Some of them set up a meeting for Cindy with two ex-Mormon Christians: a meeting that had a profound, "heart-stirring" effect on her.

Few things that happened during this period of time, though, had the devastating consequences on Cindy than did her reading about the Mormon temple ceremony. She had not gone through the temple for her endowments, choosing to wait until she was married for what she expected to be the greatest spiritual experience of her life.

One day she had occasion to look at a copy of Jerald and Sandra Tanner's book, *Mormonism, Shadow or Reality?* Though she had never felt any curiosity about any of the other contents of this book, she did turn to the section on the temple ceremony and began to read. "At first I was appalled," she recalls, "and then I began to laugh, thinking, *This can't be true—that can't possibly be the temple ceremony.*"

At that time Cindy was a close friend to a Mormon missionary serving in Southern California, a young man with whom she openly shared her experiences with the Christians who were trying to teach her. She immediately called him and briefly described what she had read in the Tanners' book.

"You've got to tell me the truth," she insisted. "Is what I read true?"

"Yes, it is," he replied. Then haltingly, he began to tell her the bittersweet "inside joke" that Mormons ask someone who has just gone through the temple for the first time: "Do you still have your testimony?"

Incredulous, Cindy called another friend, a girl who had

just been married in the temple and asked her the same question she'd asked the missionary. Her friend's admission of her own feelings of reaction to the strangeness and unbelievability of what she had seen and heard within the temple walls left Cindy aghast.

The Book of Psalms became very important to Cindy, a source of comfort and refuge as well as a mirror to her growing knowledge of, and relationship with Jesus Christ. She began to try to convey this to her seminary students, and though the class was popular and well-received, she could tell in her students' eyes that they could see no connection between these Scriptures and "the Savior" of their own experience. But the change in their teacher was obvious, even before she herself realized that the Savior and friend she was falling in love with was not the Jesus of Mormonism.

Her situation was reaching a crux of decision. One day she was overcome with emotion as a friend read passages to her from the Tanners' book. She began to weep, from deep inside herself, as she realized how critical it was that she make a decision about Mormonism. She stood up suddenly, tears flowing freely but her voice firm.

"I'm going to be able to stand before you, and before God, and tell you whether or not Mormonism is true."

Her Christian friend looked up from the book. He reached for a piece of paper that was lying beside him.

"Write that down," he said, "and date it."

"November, 1976," she wrote, and then the words she had just spoken. Her commitment endured, and like the Gilgal stones put up by the children of Israel to commemorate a passage, that worn scrap of paper is to this day a treasured memorial.

She narrowed the focus of her search: she determined to "look and see if Mormonism had the true and living Jesus Christ." Her Sunday-morning classes at the Mormon church became crowded with new people wanting to hear what she had to say about Jesus. "The funny thing was," Cindy says, "I was just teaching on Sunday morning the things I had learned the night before when I had gone with my Christian friends to their on-fire meetings."

When she was asked, shortly thereafter, to speak at a missionary-zone conference about how to win people to Mormonism, people who knew her wanted to know what was different. She didn't pray in King James English any more, but intimately, as to a friend. She addressed Jesus instead of "Heavenly Father" as she had in the past. And when she "bore her testimony," it was of a Jesus who was her lover and companion.

The young elder who had invited her to speak called her outside as soon as the meeting ended. With an earnest voice, he said, "Cindy, I know that the Mormon church is true, and that Joseph Smith was a prophet, and that Spencer W. Kimball is a prophet. But I do not know the Savior like you do."

"It was right then that God nailed me," Cindy remembers, "and the Holy Spirit let me see that I couldn't take the Jesus that I was following and was in love with, into the Mormon church. It just wouldn't work. The Jesus I was talking about was not the same as 'the Savior' the elder spoke of."

Without telling anyone, Cindy decided to conduct a private experiment. One first Sunday of the month, she went to a Fast and Testimony meeting at a ward where she knew only one person. "I kept a count of how many people bore their testimonies and what they said they were thankful for. Thirty-three people bore their testimonies that morning, and out of the 33 only three had anything to say about Jesus, other than when they ended by saying, 'In the name of Jesus Christ, amen.' Two of those three were little deacons who said by rote, 'I know that Jesus is the Christ,' and the third one was a member of the bishopric who had a little more to say on the same theme. Everybody was thankful for the church, everybody was thankful for Joseph Smith and Spencer W. Kimball, many were thankful for the *Book of Mormon*, and of course many were thankful for family and friends. But nobody testified of really knowing

Jesus Christ, and understanding what he had done for them at the cross.

"It was a real witness to me that the true and living Jesus Christ, with whom you could have a relationship, was not within the Mormon church."

In April 1977, these feelings all came to a culmination. Cindy had been removed from the job situation she had been in, partly, she says, "because of what was happening in my life and partly because of my own shortcomings at work. It was a great blow to my pride to be removed from a position by Mormons in authority over me." She had been out to dinner with a Christian friend who was telling her of his experiences during the five years that he had served as a Christian missionary in Africa. While listening with rapt attention, she felt a type of spiritual nudging: "The Lord spoke to my spirit and said, 'Get up and go home.'"

Cindy recalls looking at her watch, seeing that it was only eight o'clock, and feeling frustrated and reluctant when the message was repeated: "Be obedient. Get up and go home."

When she shared this with her friend, he was nonplussed. "It's a confirmation. Let's just kneel in prayer before you go," and they did so before she departed.

As she began to drive home, the same feeling of deep weeping came over her, the feeling she had had back in November. She became acutely aware of God's presence, and that something important was about to happen.

"As I stopped at the light at the corner of Cherry Avenue and Market," Cindy says, retracing the events of that night, "The Lord spoke to my inner self and said, *Mormonism is false.*

"I remember screaming at the top of my lungs, 'It can't be! It just can't be!' And then the message was repeated: 'Mormonism is false.'"

Cindy was shaken as she continued her drive home. She retired, setting her alarm for three hours earlier than her customary time to arise. When it sounded the next morning, she devoted herself to prayer and at the end of that time, she was left with a firm conviction that she would have to swallow her pride and admit publicly that she knew Mormonism was wrong, and that for reasons he would reveal later, she was to travel to Israel.

One seemed as impossible as the other: her great pride was every bit as big an obstacle as the lack of money for the trip.

When the Christian friend she'd had dinner with the night before came to pick her up for church, she was determined not to let him know of the decisions she'd made. She decided to respond to the altar call that evening, when she knew that her friend would be ministering elsewhere. But that morning when she arrived at the Melodyland Christian Center in Aneheim where she had been attending services, she found she was in for a change of plans.

One thing that startled her was the singing of a guest soloist, a black woman who sang fervently in a way Cindy had never before heard. This, of course, was before the 1978 pronouncement by the Mormon church that gave blacks the same privileges as whites, and in hearing that lovely singing Cindy realized for the first time "what a sin, what a debauchery, what a stench in God's nostrils it must be for me ever to think that I was better than anyone else because of the color of my skin."

Later in the service, Cindy was startled when the preacher, Ralph Wilkerson, announced that "there are five more people who God has spoken to, who need to respond. One of you knows if God has spoken to you in your car."

No doubt remained in her mind about what she needed to do. "When I went forward, I'm sure my mascara was running, my slip was probably showing, I felt completely humiliated and humbled before the cross of Jesus Christ and those Christians who had been witnessing to me. But nothing mattered but Jesus. For the first time in my life, I wanted to declare before everybody who Jesus Christ was, who he was for me, my Lord and my Savior, and that he had died for my sins: I was a sinner, in need, needing—

needing his forgiving grace and power." After a battle that had lasted a year and a half, Cindy surrendered to the King.

One of the first things she felt led by God to do was to go on a tour of Israel led by Dr. Walter Martin. The money was provided (miraculously, Cindy feels), and it was in the River Jordan that Dr. Martin baptized Cindy.

Later, at her excommunication hearing, Cindy shared with the amazed officials how she had continued to live the Word of Wisdom's health laws, how she had kept herself morally clean, and how she had learned to do more than just tithe—she had learned to give sacrificial offerings to the Lord. She shared her testimony of how she believed that Joseph Smith was a prophet—but a false one—and that her burning testimony was that of Jesus Christ and him alone.

Sheila Garrigus is petite and wide-eyed and speaks softly with a decided Mississippi accent. She tells the story of her time in Mormonism; a story that begins with the classic situation of the two fresh-faced missionaries at her door, continues with supernatural visitations, and concludes with a surrender to the person of Jesus Christ.

4

Sheila Garrigus

Sheila was born in Mobile, Alabama, in 1946, but grew up in a rural Mississippi town named Leaksville. She was firstborn in her family, but the three boys born after her all died as infants or toddlers. Bobby, only eleven months younger than she, died of leukemia at the age of four, and many of Sheila's formative religious questions centered around that devastating experience: Was her little brother in heaven or not?

She grew up struggling with the doctrine of original sin, asking questions, looking for a way to make sense of what had happened in her family. Most of the answers she got seemed unsatisfactory to her, or, as she now reflects, perhaps many were simply incorrect.

The Southern Presbyterian church she attended then was peopled, in the main, by her own relatives; even the land it sat upon had been donated by her great-great-grandfather. She worshiped there, attending Sunday morning, Sunday night, and Wednesday night, went to church camp for two weeks each summer, maturing during the American Graffiti period of Southern life.

No Mormons lived in Leaksville; in fact, none lived in the entire county. In a neighboring county there was a single Mormon family. But Sheila didn't know them, and her knowledge of Mormonism was limited to the history-book vignette in her mind of Brigham Young taking his people to Utah, where a flock of seagulls saved their endangered crops.

When Sheila went away to college to the University of Southern Mississippi at Hattiesburg, she became very active in the Presbyterian youth group on campus. She had a strong belief in a personal God, and a belief she now sees as mainly "head knowledge" concerning Jesus.

When Elder Morrison and Elder Jensen knocked at her door in September, 1966, her junior year at college, she welcomed them in. Over the next eight months she listened to their lessons, asked them questions, and finally on May 3, 1967, she was baptized into the Mormon church. There were only about five Mormon students on campus, and they became a close-knit group. Sheila shared some of her new experiences with other friends too and a close friend, Debbie Wood, was also baptized.

The reaction of Sheila's parents to her baptism was strong and negative. Her parents theorized that it was her way of "sowing wild oats," this allying of herself with this strange cult, and asked Sheila not to tell any other family members, other than her grandparents, about this act of rebellion against her heritage; in fact, to stay there at college until she had worked through this aberrant period of her life.

Sheila's response to this was to begin to pray that God would give her a "testimony." She had had none of the "burning bosom" that the *Book of Mormon* had promised would accompany her conviction that Mormonism was true, and she felt that she would never be able to withstand the family pressures unless she had some confirmational seal that what she had done in joining the Mormon church was right. Without such, she was prepared to wash her hands of the whole matter so as to "make everybody happy."

About a month and a half after her baptism, she was sitting one morning in the family room of a Mormon friend, Sister Thames. As she looked at the sun-drenched lawn, she saw someone walking across it, coming toward her. As the figure approached, she saw that it was a woman, one whom she recognized as her own Grandmother McInnes.

Only the windowpane separated the two when the grandmother began to speak. She told Sheila that she had come in response to Sheila's prayer, and that the Mormon church was the true church. Joseph Smith was indeed a prophet of God, she said, and Sheila must at all costs resist pressure from her family and stay faithful to the Mormon church, because she was the one who must do the family's genealogy work.

It looked like her grandmother—nothing ghostly or spectral—and even smelled of the fragrance that she wore. Her grandmother's familiar voice terminated the visit by telling Sheila that she herself had accepted the Mormon gospel.

Sheila sat stunned. The grandmother who had just appeared to her had been dead several years.

The result of this experience was that Sheila became completely impervious to any criticism of the Mormon church. No one could convince her that it was not of God. Such was her confidence that when she met and married handsome and personable Jim Garrigus in 1969, two years after her baptism, she felt no threat from the fact that he was a church-going Presbyterian of the same spiritual timbre as she had once been.

Today Sheila and Jim have three children, James, Jennifer, and Joshua, and are united in the Lord. She has worked for the past six years with children with learning disabilities, and she and her family are active Christians living in Atlanta, Georgia, where they worship at Eastside Baptist Church.

Point of Departure

Jim and Sheila's first major conflict occurred when their first son, James was born. Sheila wanted to have him blessed, to become a child of record in the Mormon church. Jim was surprised at Sheila's adamant insistence, and backed off from his own wishes to have their child baptized. James (Jamie) was blessed, as was his sister Jennifer when she was born some time later.

Jim and Sheila found that they could not discuss religion without conflict, so each agreed to accompany the other to social events at both the Presbyterian and Mormon churches, while they worshiped separately. Early in their marriage, Sheila agreed to discuss Mormonism with Jim's pastor, but the meetings disintegrated into arguing and were abandoned.

Three years after their marriage, Jim was transferred by his company to Arcadia, California. After the family arrived Jim became heavily involved with the Arcadia Presbyterian Church and became aware of a spiritual lack in his life. It was at this time that he made a personal commitment to Jesus Christ.

Correlative conflict heated up at home. Sheila wanted the children to continue to attend Sunday school and Primary with her, while Jim wanted them to go to the Presbyterian church with him.

It was about this time that Jim became involved in a Saturday morning men's Bible study where he met Tom Delahooke. Tom had read a great deal about Mormonism, and whenever he would talk to Sheila he would ask her questions about Mormon doctrine. Once he quoted some of Brigham Young's teaching on the Adam-God doctrine. Sheila, being "a good little Mormon," assured him that though she was not familiar with that teaching, if Brigham Young had said it, then she believed it. But when she asked her visiting teaching companion, Paula Anderson, and her home teacher about Adam's being God, they both replied with the same answer Sheila had been taught all along:

that Adam was the same as the archangel Michael. Sheila tried to push these contradictions to the back of her mind, but they continued to worry her.

Jim's pastor, Jim Hagelganz, also reached out to Sheila. He would have her come to his office once a week. She remembers him as perhaps the most gentle and loving Christian who taught her. He would tell Sheila basic Christian doctrine, what he believed, and Sheila would reply, "That's what I believe, too." But though they were using the same words and terminology, their meanings were very different and Pastor Jim became very frustrated at their lack of communication, even though they talked freely.

Sheila's husband Jim began to grow by spiritual leaps and bounds. He was attending several weekly Bible studies, and she saw his devotion to his daily, morning, private Bible study. He never said anything negative about the Mormon church to Sheila, but he had a "different spirit" about him, one that Sheila did not understand and which she saw as a personal threat.

Twin challenges arose. Tom Delahooke challenged Sheila to read the Book of John, confident that she would see there a disparity between Mormonism and Bible teaching. She read it through twice, seeing no conflicts with her own doctrine, until Tom lovingly and gently pointed out areas of conflict to her. Sheila felt an increased desire to know Mormon doctrine better and began to do more extensive reading in LDS works.

Jim's challenge, posed by Sheila, was to take the series of missionary lessons. This was the first time she had requested this of him, because she had been assured that Jim was such a nice person that she could "just love him right into the church." Sheila intensified her daily prayer for Jim: that God would show him the truth about the Mormon church. She never asked God to make him a Mormon because, she said, "I believed so wholeheartedly that the Mormon church was true and everything it said it was."

After Jim's first meeting with the young missionaries, it became apparent that they were no match for him, so they asked two stake missionaries, more mature men who were husbands of Sheila's friends, to meet with Jim. Jim dutifully met with them on Tuesday evenings. The atmosphere was friendly, discussion was relaxed. Sheila was elated. Her dream of a united family, sealed in the temple for time and all eternity, was within reach.

Wednesday mornings, though, Jim would meet with John Carlson, a Christian brother who helped Jim look up the Scripture passages he'd discussed the night before, seeing them in context, talking about their relation to the rest of the Bible.

After several weeks, Jim broke the news to Sheila: he could not accept Mormon doctrine because he saw that it conflicted in many places with the Bible, and he would never join the Mormon church. Furthermore, he wanted their son Jamie to stop attending the Mormon church and to begin attending the Presbyterian church with him.

Disbelieving, shocked, angry—Sheila was all of these. She felt more threatened than ever by Jim's new inner strength. "Our marriage became very, very rocky at that point," she says, "but Jim knows me very well." Instead of more direct conflict, Jim appealed to Sheila's love of reading and went to a religious bookstore and bought stacks of books. None were about Mormonism; instead, they were books of personal testimony and strength by people like David Wilkerson and George Otis and Pat Boone. Jim put them on his nightstand, knowing that Sheila would read them too.

And read them she did. "I was enjoying them, because I didn't feel in any way threatened by them. The Lord used these books to minister to me, because as I was reading about God's power in these people's lives, I realized that they had something in their lives that I did not have in mine. I believed that the Holy Ghost was found only in the Mormon church and yet these people had power and joy that I did not have, and did not see in my LDS friends. This bothered me greatly."

She saw, too, that her entire spiritual focus was on God the Father, to the exclusion in worship and in prayer of Jesus Christ. She began to wonder about her relationship with Jesus. Jim's only comment to her during this time of great turmoil was a gentle one: "You know *about* him, but you do not *know* him."

Sheila began to pray earnestly about these apparent paradoxes, her deteriorating marriage, her confusion, her dashed hopes of Jim becoming a Mormon. One night in February 1975, while Jim was away on a business trip in Alaska, Sheila began to pray, as she always had, to Heavenly Father. But feelings of turmoil and frustration and even anger overwhelmed her. So she began again.

"Jesus," she prayed, "I believe I know you. I believe I worship you, but I know that if I don't really know who you are, as Jim said, I would like to know you in the same way that Jim seems to know you. And if you are indeed standing, knocking at the door of my heart, then right now, I'm opening that door. You are welcome to come in. You can take my marriage, my life, you can take all this confusion, all of this anger, all of this frustration, and straighten it out. I give it to you."

She arose from her knees and went to bed. She didn't feel any different, but when Jim returned from his trip, he told her that he sensed something different in her. His Valentine gifts to her a few days later were *The Living Bible* and a pact to read from the Bible each day, whether separately or together. Sheila agreed.

A few days later a little German lady, Hilde Lutton, knocked on Sheila's door. She had gone to each house in the neighborhood, inviting people to a nondenominational Bible study. Sheila and Jim became involved in Hilde and Bob's study of the Book of John, and also a study of the Book of Philippians in the home of John and Rosalee Carlson.

In ways that were at the time imperceptible to her, Sheila began to change. The first Mormon doctrine she rejected as a result of her study of the Bible was the doctrine of eternal progression: "The more I learned about Jesus, I realized that I could never become a goddess." But she still felt bound emotionally to the Mormon church, and to her dream of having her family united throughout eternity.

Sheila began to share her dilemma with her bishop, and when she told him of Jim's final decision not to become a Mormon, the bishop made an appointment to meet with both of them in their home.

"Jim has made a sincere decision," the bishop said, "and now you, Sheila, need to make a decision. There are three choices open to you. The first choice is that you could divorce Jim, because you as a believer should not be yoked with a nonbeliever gentile. As much as I like Jim, this is a real choice for you.

"Your second choice is to remain married to Jim for a time, stay in the church and raise your children in the church. At the time of your death, you will become a ministering angel.

"Or, you can stay married, remain faithful to the church, and at the time of your death you can be vicariously sealed to a LDS man in the temple as his second or third wife."

Sheila loved Jim and did not want to divorce him. But she did not want to be a ministering angel either, so she chose the third option. She believed that her children and she could continue to be a family unit in the Celestial Kingdom with another man. "It would be as if Jim never existed," she reflects, "but such was my belief in the church, and my bond to it, that I chose the third choice."

At her bishop's urging, she dropped out of her Bible studies, but she felt so hungry for the Word that she soon returned to personal and group study. But her feelings that others were saying that she could not be a Christian and a Mormon made her angry—so angry, in fact, that she demanded a divorce from Jim. In blistering prayer the next day, she told God not to make her choose between Jesus and the Mormon church, because her mind was made up: she chose the church.

Again she turned away from the Bible and the fellowship of Christians. And again she felt the recurrent hunger not only for the Bible, but for the person of the Bible: Jesus.

She took a spiritual inventory and found herself emptier than before. She realized that her Mormon friends could not help her in this situation, for they were just as deceived as she felt herself to be. And Christians, loving though they might be, could not identify with her feelings. She began to pray earnestly that God would send someone into her life who was not only a Christian, but who could understand her Mormon background from personal experience.

The next day Jim attended his weekly Christian Business Men's Committee Breakfast, and the scheduled speaker did not show up. Each of the men stood and shared something on his heart, and when Jim explained his need to contact an ex-Mormon Christian, another man present at the meeting arranged for Sheila to meet Jerry and Marion Bodine, who in turn introduced her to John Henry Yount, a former temple worker who was now a Christian.

"He knew what I felt. He knew how difficult it was. And he was so understanding, and helped me know what I needed to do."

In one of the hardest and most courageous acts of her life, Sheila knelt and told God that she was sorry that she had been involved in the Mormon church. "I told him that I knew that it was like a slap in the face to him," she recalls, "and that I knew for the first time that the Mormon god, and the Mormon Jesus, and Mormon theology were false—a lie—and that by believing it and practicing it I had blasphemed, and that I was sorry for that."

In July, Sheila wrote a letter to her bishop requesting that her name and those of her two children be removed from the rolls of the Mormon church. A bishop's court was held on November 2, 1976, in which her request was granted.

She cuts an unmistakable figure, this sweet-faced septuagenarian in her ankle-length pioneer dress and sunbonnet as she moves through crowds of Mormons near Temple Square in Salt Lake City. Her "tracting apron," a ruffled version of a sandwich board, is emblazoned with a picture of her ancestor, John D. Lee, and the question, *"Who is this man . . . and why did he have nineteen wives and sixty-four children?"*

Her story of growing up with the dream of becoming a goddess and queen in her own heaven has now been replaced with tireless servanthood here for the King of kings.

5

Thelma "Granny" Geer

When Thelma Rachael Smithson was born into the tiny Mormon community of Lebanon (better known to locals as Cactus Flat), Arizona, her birth fulfilled for her mother and father the ambition of providing a Mormon home and a white body for another one of the "Mormon god's" spirit children.[1]

Little Thelma grew up completely enmeshed in Mormonism. She was baptized and confirmed a member of the church at age eight. She learned its doctrines as few converts can: not only from church lesson manuals and teachers, but also as a heritage from her own family. Her paternal great-grandfather, John D. Lee, was a notorious figure in history. He and "fifty or sixty" other Mormon elders had led a band of conscripted Utah Indians in the slaughter of 127 fellow Americans at Mountain Meadows, Utah.[2]

Twenty years later, as the lone scapegoat for the priest-plotted Mountain Meadows Massacre, he was excommunicated by the Mormon Church, turned over to a United States firing squad and shot to death at Mountain Meadows. One hundred years later the Mormon Church posthumously pardoned him and restored all his former blessings.[3]

The stories of how, by the powers of the Mormon priesthood, sixteen of John D. Lee's nineteen wives had been given in eternal marriage to other LDS elders and one hundred years later restored to him by the powers of the same Mormon priesthood were sobering to the young girl as she listened intently to the chilling accounts. And sobering they should have been, especially the accounts her grandmother shared of how and why LDS men were "blood-atoned" (killed) for certain grievous sins, and "covenant-breaking."[4]

Thelma's concept of God, the glorified man of Mormon doctrine, pervaded her waking hours. She wondered, even as a young girl, how the Mormon "god" in his physical body could be in the bridal chambers begetting myriads of "spirit babies" and yet be aware of the prayers of a little Mormon lass far away on the earth.

Thelma's loving concerns especially included her purported "Heavenly Mother." In reverie and in song she glorified Mormonism's "Heavenly Mother":

> In the heavens are parents single?
> No, the thought makes reason stare.
> Truth is reason, truth eternal
> Tells me I've a Mother there.
>   "Oh, My Father," *LDS Hymnal*

Thelma grew up with yet another peculiar LDS view. She recalls that she was taught to look down on all dark-complexioned people. For according to Mormonism, a dark skin is the "mark" denoting sin in a purported pre-existence or in the lives of ancestors.[5]

Thelma believed, as all devout Mormons do, that it would be her responsibility to provide mortal bodies for as many as possible of the little "spirit-children" in heaven that God the Father and his wives—"Heavenly Mothers"—were procreating.[6] She looked forward to marrying a Mormon elder in a Mormon temple and bearing a multitude of children on earth and in heaven. All Mormons (and non-Mormons) who do not marry in the Mormon "House of the Lord" will be eternal servants to those who do.

"Well-meant assurances that even the servants would be happy in this celestialized Mormon earth-heaven did not impress me or deter me from my set goal," Granny Geer recalls. "I was determined to marry early and to marry well. My prospective bridegroom-god was already picked out. Someone else could wash the dishes, do the dydees, and the numerous other household chores in heaven: I intended to be a queen in heaven, not a servant."[7]

Her hope chest contained only one item: a little hand-made baby quilt. All she lacked was a husband and she didn't want to date anyone but a Mormon. But she didn't allow for that unpredictable variable of "chemistry." When she met handsome and gentle non-Mormon Ernest Geer at a Mormon dance, they fell in love and were soon married.

Since Ernest was not a Christian, he easily tolerated Thelma's attendance at the local Mormon Church and her fantasies of Ernest succumbing to Mormonism so he could become a "god" and she could be a "goddess." For her part, Thelma did not worry overmuch that her "Honey" was not a Mormon when they married. She knew from statistics that seven out of ten non-Mormon mates are coerced and "diverted" into Mormonism by their spouses. And so she expectantly set herself (as all good Mormon wives should) to homemaking, raising a family, and helping her husband make a living in her Mormon-dominated hometown, Safford, Arizona. She was confident that Ernest would soon be converted.

(Ernest was indeed converted—to Christ and Christianity—one week after Thelma was! And Thelma still teases him that "it took a Mormon to make a Christian out of you.")

Point of Departure

Thelma and Ernest had been married just eight years and were still unsaved when her beloved papa died. Because he had lived as a "jack Mormon," using tea, coffee, and tobacco, and refusing to pay his tithe, he had been denied the Mormon temple ordinances, particularly the most essential "marriage for eternity." He had died fully expecting to go to Mormonism's temporary "prison-place for disobedient spirits,"[8] but anticipating that Joseph Smith would soon allow Papa to progress on in the "spirit world." There Papa would prepare a place for Mama and their four children and their progeny so that "where he is, we may be also." Meanwhile, Mama was to strictly observe Mormonism's Word of Wisdom, the dietary laws, pay the back tithes, and journey to the Arizona temple. There a Mormon elder would "stand in" Papa's place to receive vicarious washings and anointings. The elder would don LDS "holy garments" including the sacred, protective temple underwear, so that priesthood ordinations could be performed on Papa's behalf. Mama meanwhile would be washed and anointed and then would put on sacred LDS bridal garments—underwear, wedding gown, and veil. Then, finally, by the power of the holy Mormon priesthood, Mama and Papa could be married and sealed for eternity, and enabled to keep on having children in heaven. They would thus attain Mormonism's ultimate goal of becoming a "god" and a "goddess."[9]

As the years hurried by, Thelma's hopes of "diverting" Ernest into Mormonism dimmed. But she took comfort in the Mormon doctrine that after Ernest's death she could have vicarious baptism and priesthood ordinations performed in the Mormon temple for him. And, finally, she could be married to him for eternity. When she herself died, Thelma and her now-Mormon husband Ernest could beget eternities of children to populate their own earth(s) and thus Ernest would become a Mormon "god" and Thelma a "goddess."

But some of her childhood worries kept returning to plague her. If she would be living with Papa and Mama on Papa's planet-heaven, how could she be with Ernest and their children on their own planet-heaven? Ernest assertedly would form his own world out of preexisting materials as Adam purportedly had formed this earth for his wives and posterity.[10] Her musings brought on other speculations about how much time Mormonism's fleshly-bodied God must have to spend in the bridal chambers with his polygamist wives, busily procreating spirit bodies for the demons, angels, Jesus, Lucifer, the Holy Ghost, and for every person who has ever lived and will live on this earth. With that thought came the aching yearnings of her childhood: Was that why God took so long to respond to the prayers of a little girl in the Arizona desert? No wonder he seemed so far away, too busy to hear and answer her prayers.

When she had asked her mother about such "mysteries," Thelma discovered two things: her mother did not understand them either, and furthermore, she was not willing or allowed to discuss them.

Thelma was nearly thirty-one years old when a Christian tract came in the mail. She read about another mystery, one that was to her just as incomprehensible. It said that Jesus had died for her sins. Thelma shook her head in disbelief as she read: *You must be born again!* She wondered, *What does it mean to be born again?* She read and reread the pamphlet and then carefully laid it on the cupboard shelf where it could be picked up and read again and again.

The months that followed were rough financially for the Geers. They picked cotton for a living, alongside Ernest's father, Major Andrew Geer. As they worked, Grandpa Geer would sing songs much different from the ones Thelma's mother used to sing. He sang about Jesus, the

Lamb of God. Thelma listened carefully as he sang, "Jesus paid it all, all to him I owe."

Major Andrew Geer had migrated to Arizona as a share-cropper from East Texas. He was proud of his Christian forebears and his charter membership in the newly organized Calvary Baptist Church. He was a gentle man, but persistent in his pleadings that his son and family attend church with him.

In mid-December Thelma finally decided that she would accompany Grandpa Geer to the Baptist Church a time or two. She thought that if she accompanied him to his church, he and his son would feel obligated to accompany her to the Mormon Church. Then Ernest would become a Mormon and Thelma's dreams would come true.

But Thelma's connivings backfired. As she listened to and eventually joined in the enthusiastic singing of the Christmas carols and other gospel songs, the Holy Spirit convicted her that "These people love and honor Jesus in a way that I have never loved and honored him."

She listened with interest—and mounting anger—to a sermon which insisted that "all men were conceived in sin and brought forth in iniquity." On the way home she bristled to her father-in-law and Ernest, "That preacher can say he's a child of Satan if he wants to but when I was born on earth, I was already a child of God. When we get home I'll prove to you from the Bible that all people, plus Jesus, Satan, all the angels, and even the Holy Ghost were born in heaven to God and to our Heavenly Mothers."[11]

To her dismay, Thelma could find none of these Mormon teachings in the Bible. But, still confident and determined, she assured Ernest, "We can find proof in the Mormon scriptures."

Ernest put his foot down, "I'll read the Bible with you all day if that's what it takes, but I won't help you look for anything in your bogus Mormon 'scriptures.'" To her chagrin Thelma could not find even one mention in her Mormon scriptures of "Heavenly Mothers" or "spirit babies." But to her consternation and surprise, she was led by the Holy Spirit to the astounding fact that both the Bible and the Book of Mormon state that Jesus came in the "fullness of time."[12] However, Mormonism's other two "scriptures," the *Doctrine and Covenants* and the *Pearl of Great Price* assert that Jesus came in the "meridian of time."

"Which should I believe? Here are four books I believe to be divinely inspired but two disagree with the other two." Thelma was confused. Under the gentle persuasion of the Holy Spirit, Thelma was led to read only the Bible.

She soon learned that Jesus paid for all sin on the cross, not in the Garden of Gethsemane, as Mormonism teaches.[13] Longing to know more about Jesus, Thelma continued to attend Calvary Baptist Church. At this Christmas season she discovered for the first time the true meaning of the virgin birth. She remembers that, "My heart was burdened. I felt guilty for attending the Baptist services and especially ashamed for enjoying them. For according to *Joseph Smith's Own Story*, "all other churches . . . were all wrong . . . all their creeds were an abomination in His sight . . . their professors were all corrupt."[14]

Thelma continued, "Moreover, I was deeply disturbed to realize and admit my beloved Mormon Church opposed certain biblical truths, especially the truths about Jesus and his virgin birth."[15] Remembering Joseph Smith's admonition that it is an old sectarian false notion that Jesus can dwell in a man's heart, Thelma struggled with her thoughts. How could Jesus have preeminence in her heart if he could not dwell there? She longed to respond to the Baptist pastor's invitation to open her heart to Jesus.

Now, after thirty-one years of longing to know more about Jesus, her hungry soul was being fed, her heart was being strangely stirred as it had never been before. On the first Sunday morning of January, 1947, Thelma answered the invitation and in simple childlike faith prayed the prayer, "Please come into my heart and show me how to give you preeminence, Jesus." The next Sunday Ernest made a public commitment to his Savior, and the following Sunday morning their twelve-year-old Jacqueline received Jesus. On the fourth Sunday in January the three were baptized.

Notes

1. *Mormonism, Mama, and Me*, p. 25, 186, 267. See also Fielding Smith, *The Way to Perfection*, p. 48; Apostle Orson Pratt, *Journal of Discourses*, vol. 16, p. 334.

2. *Mormonism, Mama, and Me*, pp. 161–68.

3. *Mormonism, Mama, and Me*, pp. 168–71.

4. *Mormonism, Mama, and Me*, pp. 127–60, 258–64; *Journal of Discourses*, vols. 1, 4, 10.

5. *Mormonism, Mama, and Me*, pp. 219–351 *Book of Mormon*, 3; Nephi 2:15; *Pearl of Great Price:* Book of Abraham, 1:21–27; Book of Moses, 7:8; *The Juvenile Instructor*, vol. 26, p. 635; vol. 30, p. 129; B. Young, *Journal of Discourses*, 10:110.

6. *Mormonism, Mama, and Me*, p. 74–5, 86, 96, 98, 267–69.

7. Kimball, *Journal of Discourses*, vol. 3; p. 109, McConkie, *Mormon Doctrine*, p. 670; Joseph Fielding Smith, *The Way to Perfection*, pp. 249–50.

8. *Mormonism, Mama, and Me*, pp. 108, 197; N. B. Lundwall, "The Vision," pp. 59–60; B. Young, *Journal of Discourses*, vol. 7.

9. *Mormonism, Mama, and Me*, p. 197; *Gospel Principles*, pp. 213, 234, 236.

10. *Mormonism, Mama, and Me*, pp. 96, 100, 250–51; *Millennial Star*, No. 48, vol. XV; B. Young, *Journal of Discourses*, vol. 1, p. 50.

11. *Mormonism, Mama, and Me*, pp. 18, 71, 96, 187; B. H. Roberts, *New Witness for God*, p. 461 [1895]; B. Young, *Journal of Discourses*, vol. 1, pp. 50–1; Orson Hyde, *Journal of Discourses*, vol. 2, p. 210.

12. *Mormonism, Mama, and Me*, pp, 43–44.

13. *Mormonism, Mama, and Me*, p. 188 (Uniform System for Teaching Families, Discussion 1, p. 56).

14. Joseph Smith, *Pearl of Great Price*, 2:19.

15. *Mormonism, Mama, and Me*, p. 86–96, 250; Brigham Young, *Journal of Discourses*, vol. 4, p. 218; O. Pratt, *The Seer*, pp. 2, 158; Bruce McConkie, *Mormon Doctrine*, p. 547, 742; Bruce McConkie, *The Promised Messiah*, p. 468.

Even at the age of 30, Kevin Bond still has the fresh-scrubbed look, direct eye contact, and frank voice that made him a successful missionary for the Mormon church years before. It was while he was on his mission in Albuquerque, New Mexico, that Kevin first confronted realities about the gospel he was presenting to others, and now his new mission field—the hearts of his Mormon family and friends in Utah—presents new challenges that will last a lifetime.

6

Kevin Bond

Kevin Bond was born in 1960 in Orville, California. His parents, Donald R. and Constance Ann Bond, were both converts to the Mormon church. His mother came from a Baptist heritage, and his father actually "tracted out" and converted Kevin's mother and her family.

This marriage produced seven children: a son Steven, identical twins Kevin and Kris, and four others. The Bonds taught their children strong ethical standards, and emphasized that each one should believe wholeheartedly his convictions, and act upon them.

Twins Kevin and Kris were baptized the same day in 1968, in a font just beneath the Tabernacle on Temple Square in Salt Lake City. Kevin recalls that a great motivating factor in his personality, that of obedience, was the impetus for that act. "Even from that time," recalls Kevin, "my foundation has always been on the person of Jesus Christ and my relationship with God, separate from any organization. I think that growing up I was able to see past the ritualism and legalities of Mormonism because I focused beyond them, going on long walks, talking to God."

His life was nonetheless an active one in the church. His father spearheaded many of the home-study programs for the church's youth education, seminaries, and institutes; and was responsible for implementing the education program in Fiji and Tonga. His father has served as seminary teacher, bishop, and on the Stake Council, and his mother has for many years sung with the Mormon Tabernacle Choir. There was a constant air of "busyness," Kevin reminisces, an atmosphere in which their large family flourished, and in which young Kevin grew and took part in all the church programs and activities.

"I was on fire for the Mormon church," Kevin says, "and I always listened carefully in Sunday School, always anxious to hear the Shepherd's voice."

Even his moments of teenage rebellion had limits. One evening in his late teens, after what he terms a "rowdy" period, Kevin felt a void that drove him to prayer, asking God to lead him, to direct him. The resultant sense of communication, of being led, set a precedent for Kevin. This, along with the love he had for his father—a love that had a tether on it that kept Kevin from straying too far—were stabilizing influences in his young life

When Kevin left on his mission in 1980, he was a little older than most young men when they leave. His motivation for going was a strong sense of obedience and sense of duty, and he had waited until he felt that he was ready. While being trained for his mission, Kevin felt an immediate aversion to the highly regimented manner of teaching the memorized lessons. He felt it stifled not only the motivation of the missionaries, but also any inspiration that the missionary might otherwise receive.

"I did it my own way," Kevin says, "I told people what I knew. I think people saw that here was a guy who doesn't claim to know all the answers, who will find out for us anything he doesn't know." His approach was successful: his mission district led the nation in baptisms, and during one summer Kevin was its most prolific baptizer.

To many of those people that he influenced for Mormonism, Kevin has written letters that convey not only his apology for the false things he taught them, but also convey his excitement like that of Andrew when he told Peter, "Come, come, I have found the Messiah!" (*see* John 1:41). Today Kevin is a Christian. He lives with his wife, Michelle, and son, Matthew, in Salt Lake City, Utah, where he is attending the University of Utah. Since the death last summer of his twin, Kris, who succumbed to an undiagnosed heart defect, Kevin has undergone surgery to correct the same defect in his own heart.

Point of Departure

While Kevin was on his mission, several incidents occurred that led to his departure from the Mormon church.

The first of these took place when Kevin and his companion were visiting a Protestant church, the denomination of which he does not even remember. But he does remember vividly sitting in the pew, watching a film about Jesus and hearing the message of the cross, powerfully preached.

"Immediately I started feeling this burning in my bosom," he says, "and anyone who knows Mormon testimony recognizes that as the test of truth. I stopped right there and thought, *Wait a minute. Something is wrong here. Here I am in a Protestant congregation and I'm feeling convinced it is truth.*" He decided at that point that there had to be another standard or test of truth besides feelings, and he began to look for more concrete ways in which he was convinced God could lead.

Some time later he and a companion were "tracting"—going from door-to-door to try to set up studies. A very large man had passed them, walking to his home, and as they rang his doorbell a few minutes later, they were unprepared for his greeting. "In Jesus' name," he thundered, his body filling the entire door frame, "I rebuke you and I rebuke your mission!"

Kevin recalls a flash of red coming across his vision— not anger, just an unexplained sensation—as he struggled to regain his composure. Then his sense of humor surfaced.

"What are we supposed to do now, sir? Keel over and die?"

A nervous laugh escaped his companion. Kevin continued, "I invite you in the name of Jesus Christ to hear our message."

"The Jesus that you do not know!" the man replied.

"No, *you* do not know Jesus," Kevin deflected. The exchange ended there, but Kevin's reflection on it did not. He had thought he could be prepared for such an experience, but the authority with which the man had said those words ate at him like a slow-acting acid.

At one point on his mission Kevin was confined to bed for a week because of concurrent attacks of bronchitis and bursitis. He decided to spend his time reading straight through the *Doctrine and Covenants.* "Something about it unsettled me," Kevin remembers. "It didn't sound like the Shepherd's voice. It was cluttered with gimme, gimme, gimme."

Kevin prayed fervently about this disturbing sensation, and asked a friend for help. The friend gave him a commentary which, instead of answering questions, just led him to the conclusion that what he saw in the *Doctrine and Covenants* was foreign to the first-century message of the Good Shepherd he was seeking.

But Kevin was still on his mission, and wanted to return home honorably to his family, having completed his term of duty. He kept his doubts to himself and began to voraciously read as much Mormon history as he could get his hands on. This became a substitute for the daily devotionals of *Book of Mormon* or other church "scripture" reading.

Added to these—his reading and his changing feelings—was the influence of a short, bespectacled blond Baptist lady by the name of Jane Tallant in Albuquerque who befriended him and his companion, Doug Neidrick.

She invited them over for meals, took them gifts of food and reading materials, called them on the phone. She told all her friends about Kevin and Doug, browbeating those friends into commitments to pray for the two missionaries. Some of those friends thought she was wasting her time, and some told her so. Jane's fervency, or "burden," as she called it, didn't make sense to people around her, for after all, everybody knew that you can't convert a Mormon while he is on his mission.

"At that time, we saw her as a confrontation, a conflict," Kevin recalls. "She had never-ending, unexpendable energy. But there was something in her that was very genuine, and we loved her. She reasoned with us, using Scripture, and did it reverently and gently. She not only told us what she believed, but showed us why from the Word, and then told us of her great desire that we see it, too."

She also introduced Kevin to the books about Mormonism written by Walter Martin, John L. Smith, Floyd McElveen, and Latayne Scott. "I remember skimming through them with Jane," Kevin says, "and looking up Scriptures with her."

But when Kevin moved away from New Mexico and returned home from his mission, other things were on his mind. He met and married a blond-haired young Mormon woman who was as devout as she was pretty—and she was beautiful.

Kevin and his bride, Michelle, were active in church, the model family. But Kevin began to wrestle more actively with his doubts, which fell into three categories:

The Adam-God Theory. Kevin's extensive reading of church history had convinced him that Brigham Young had indeed taught that Adam and God were one and the same. "I didn't feel that Brigham Young knew God," Kevin says. "I couldn't follow someone who was making more claims than he could back up—who showed an ignorance of Scripture, historical Christianity, and sound doctrine."

The *Book of Mormon*. Kevin concluded that much of it had been plagiarized from the Bible, and began to suspect that if a computer comparison of the two were made, that there would be little extra-biblical material in the *Book of Mormon*. If it provided little "new" information, he reasoned, why was it here? And if the Bible were indeed faulty, why use it to "prove" the *Book of Mormon*?

The *Pearl of Great Price*. "It seemed to me to be blatant evidence of Joseph Smith's being caught in a lie. But how could it be so deceptive and still be a part of my religion?"

Added to these three factors was the fact that he had "written off" the *Doctrine and Covenants* as inspired revelation years before on his mission. These gone, he began increasingly to turn to the Bible for help. Once, while on his mission, he had received special, supernatural help from the Bible, and its importance in his life continued to grow.

This was reflected in his teachings. As his teaching responsibilities in the Mormon church increased, so did his dependence on Bible Scriptures, not those of Mormonism. At one point he threw away his Triple Combination—a leather-bound volume containing the *Book of Mormon*, the *Doctrine and Covenants*, and the *Pearl of Great Price*.

His wife, Michelle, was aghast. She pled with him, crying, knowing that this was a symptom of something much deeper. She called his father and wanted to have him speak to Kevin, and tried to set up appointments with General Authorities of the church.

One evening after Michelle and Matthew had retired, Kevin stayed up, alone. He felt, he remembers, "a tremendous yearning to find God."

The events that transpired there and the accompanying feelings of resolution and peace caused a difference that Michelle immediately remarked on. "It was a miraculous change," she says, and one that both threatened and strengthened her. Though she sensed that the entire super-structure of her lifestyle was in danger, she also could not deny the transformation in Kevin, his newfound peace and courage.

After much soul searching, Kevin and Michelle resigned from the Mormon church in late 1985. Michelle accepted the Lord some six months later.

As a young Mormon girl growing up in Southern California, Sandra Tanner was definitely in the minority in her school. It wasn't until she was in the sixth grade that a Jewish girl came to the all-Protestant school, providing Sandra with a playmate who understood what it was like to be "different." Now, years later, this sandy-haired, unpretentious woman is again in the minority—she and her husband are probably the most famous and influential ex-Mormon Christians in the history of the Mormon church, and they live and work just minutes away from Mormon Church Headquarters, in the heart of Salt Lake City.

7

Sandra Tanner

Sandra Tanner was born in 1941 at an LDS hospital in Salt Lake City. Her parents, both devout Mormons, had been married in the Salt Lake City Temple, and gave their second-born child a heritage with roots deep in the Mormon faith. Sandra's mother's name was Young, and her newborn child was a great-great granddaughter of Brigham Young. Sandra's father's line, of near-fanatical converts to Mormonism, was even more devoted to Mormonism than was the Young line.

Shortly after her birth, Sandra's family moved to Southern California, where her father had a job in defense work. There, away from the Utah culture, her parents became less active in the church, though they made sure that Sandra was baptized at age eight, and she attended Primary sporadically. The San Fernando Valley where they made their home, however, was heavily Catholic, and much of her instruction involved teaching against the Catholics, who, she was told, "hid their books and burned their Bibles and don't know their history."

Mormons, she learned, were proud of their history. "I was raised on fantastic stories about Brigham Young," Sandra recalls. "His son, Brigham Young, Junior, who was also an apostle, was my great-grandfather, and one of his last plural wives, my great-grandmother, was still alive when I was young." This venerable old woman told wide-eyed Sandra hair-raising stories of how her great-grandfather continued to live in polygamy long after it was outlawed. God protected those who obeyed him in spite of civil laws, she would say, and she had many an account of how Brigham Junior had escaped sheriffs through hiding or subterfuge or masquerade.

Because her family had to drive past a Reorganized Church of Jesus Christ of Latter Day Saints each week on their way to Sunday School, Sandra knew there were "other kinds of Mormons" (a fact that seemed strange to her), and knew that some of her own relatives had left her church for other faiths: an uncle had gone into the B'hai religion, and a cousin who had married an exchange student from Iran had become a Muslim.

By the time Sandra reached junior high school, she was the motivating religious influence in her family, encouraging her mother and father to attend church before their trips to the beach. She became very active in Mutual and in the church's Seminary program.

"I was completely happy and satisfied as a Mormon," Sandra remembers. "I kept the Word of Wisdom, taught Sunday School, and thoroughly enjoyed the Mormon activities."

As her interest increased, her mother's seemed to take another track. Sandra recalls coming home many days after school and finding papers and history books (among them *No Man Knows My History* by Fawn Brodie) that her mother had ordered from Salt Lake City strewn all over the front room. Her single-minded interest in the history of Mormonism seemed to overshadow everything else in her life.

This was irritating to Sandra. Her mother would always ask her what she had learned in seminary, and when Sandra would relate the morning's lesson, her mother always had questions. She insisted that Sandra ask her seminary teacher, who would patiently tell Sandra to go home and pray, that God would give her the answers to tell her mother.

Her mother was also a topic of conversation at church, because she insisted on looking up scriptures as they were read ("What? You don't trust the manual? You have to look up everything?") and asked so many questions in Gospel Doctrine class that a man there stood up and shook his fist at her, quoting the scripture about the wicked and adulterous nation seeking after a sign.

"Mother sort of took that as a hostile feeling," Sandra laughs, remembering that her mother went from there to the missionary class where she was soon asked to leave because her questions were disturbing the "investigators" who attended it.

Sandra, meanwhile, was embarrassed and confused by her mother's actions. Even when her questions made sense, and had no logical answers in Mormonism, Sandra wanted to put them aside.

In 1957 while she was in the tenth grade, Sandra's Seminary class went to the dedication of the Los Angeles Temple. There, in a special ceremony that involved the waving of white handkerchiefs and the chanting of a "hosanna shout," Sandra was struck by the contrast between this and the mundane, orderly Mormon services to which she was so accustomed. Her bishop later deflected her questions, telling her that she wasn't to speak of such things outside the temple.

When she enrolled in Institute of Religion classes at college, Sandra felt sure, though, that some of her mother's questions that stubbornly remained in her mind would be

answered by a college-trained teacher. Her feelings of combined *déjà vu* and hurt were overwhelming when the
Institute teacher asked her to stop asking so many questions because she was disturbing a non-Mormon in the
class.

"The questions were disturbing me, too," Sandra recalls.

About the end of April the following year, Sandra traveled to Salt Lake City to spend a long weekend with her
grandmother Young. While she was there, her grandmother asked Sandra to take her to a religious meeting across
town, one which she thought Sandra would be interested
in. When Sandra knocked at the door, a tall, handsome,
dark-haired young man answered the door, and ushered
her not only into a meeting she didn't expect, but into a life
she would never have dreamed.

That young man, Jerald Tanner, and Sandra are married
and have worshiped at the same Christian fellowship in
Salt Lake City for almost twenty-five years. The publishing
company they founded, Utah Lighthouse Ministry (formerly Modern Microfilm), has for many years provided an
invaluable service by reproducing early Mormon documents, much to the gratitude of not only Christians, but
also Mormon historians who often were unable to obtain
the documents from their own church.

Point of Departure

There were incidents that occurred before Sandra met
Jerald that she believes were used by God to prepare her
mind for what he would tell her. In particular, her mother's persistent questions about the history of Mormonism
as well as its doctrines were formative in her thinking,
although she did not realize it at the time.

Sandra recalls though that the very first challenge to her
beliefs occurred in junior high school. There a friend in
gym class asked Sandra about the Mormon concept of
God. Sandra was delighted with being able to share some
of what she believed with this girl who came from a strong

Protestant home, and struggled with finding just the right way to explain the Mormon God to her friend. Then she remembered a saying she had been taught.

"As God once was," she recited, "man now is. And as God is, man may become." She stopped, pleased with finding such a neat way to make her point.

Her friend stared at her with open-mouthed amazement "Sandra," she said, "that's blasphemy!"

It was Sandra's turn to stare, this time at her friend who walked away from her, and who refused ever again to talk with Sandra about religion.

A few summers later, Sandra became acquainted with neighbors who were Jehovah's Witnesses, and listened carefully as they presented several lessons about Jehovah and Elohim. "I wasn't at all interested in becoming a Jehovah's Witness," Sandra says, "but I was interested in what made them 'tick.'"

When the summer (and the lessons) concluded, Sandra found to her delight that the subject being covered in Seminary the next year was to be the Old Testament. Her studies of the summer spawned questions about the Mormon doctrine that says that Jehovah is Jesus Christ, the God of the Old Testament; and Elohim is God the Father. And of course her mother exacerbated her distress by pointing out that the term LORD God which appeared throughout the Old Testament actually consisted of both names.

During Sandra's high school years, her mother had enrolled her younger brother in a private school. The fact that it was a Christian school was something her mother was willing to overlook because of the quality of education he was receiving there. Once when a special program was announced at the church that housed the school, Sandra and her mother went.

The meeting turned out to be one that featured a visiting evangelist who preached a lesson from a Bible text, and then sang spiritual songs with his wife.

"I was impressed with their joy, the genuineness of their

commitment to God," Sandra remembers, "which contrast-
ed with what I had often been told about Christian minis-
ters—that they weren't sincere, and were just in it for the
money and the prestige."

The message, however, went right over Sandra's head.
"It might as well have been in Chinese," she says, "because
I couldn't understand the language and the vocabulary the
minister was using. I had never heard any of the songs
before. Everything in that service was foreign to me."

Though she was impressed with the positive atmosphere, she had no desire to return. Her curiosity, like that
she once had about the Jehovah's Witnesses, was now satisfied, and she was quite content to return to her familiar
Mormon ward.

It was not until she met Jerald Tanner at the meeting her
Grandmother Young had wanted to attend that Sandra
again had any real brushes with Christianity. At this meeting Jerald was playing an audio tape of the testimony of a
woman who had left the Reorganized LDS Church.

Jerald's teenage years had been quite different from
Sandra's. Though raised as a Mormon, he had become
inactive, and had gone the more rebellious route of drinking and smoking; and it was not until he became of age to
go on a mission that he decided that he should straighten
out his life and get ready for "the call." He had come into
contact with a Reorganized LDS Church whose pastor
spent a long time showing Jerald the errors in the Utah
church with the hopes of converting him to the
Reorganized Church.

At the time Jerald and Sandra met, Jerald had become
convinced that Joseph Smith was at one time indeed a
prophet, but that he had "fallen"; and while Jerald
believed the *Book of Mormon* to be true, any of the later doctrines of the Utah church—degrees of heaven, plurality of
gods, preexistence, and so forth—Jerald regarded as false.

This was a new thought for Sandra, but when she invited him over the next night to her grandmother's, she was
more interested in the man than the message. He brought

stacks of books and returned again and again to explain to her what conclusions he had reached. It was not until Sandra realized that he might discover the shallowness of her own knowledge of Mormon scripture that she decided to do some investigating on her own.

Sandra went to a bookstore and bought a copy of the *Book of Commandments*, which is an early edition of the *Doctrine and Covenants*. She first read all the way through her own *Doctrine and Covenants* (discovering in this initial reading several elements whose falseness made her very uncomfortable) and then she and her grandmother devised a plan. They spent several days in which Sandra would read a section from the *Book of Commandments* and then her grandmother would read the corresponding section from the *Doctrine and Covenants*. Sandra carefully marked in the margins the hundreds of changes they found, and by the end of the study, Sandra had posed a disturbing question: Couldn't the God of the universe get things straight the first time, without having to completely revise his revelations?

Shortly thereafter, Jerald asked Sandra if she would like to read some of Brigham Young's sermons. She breathed a sigh of relief—here at last she would be on safe ground, for wasn't Brigham Young her own flesh and blood?

Jerald brought over to her several volumes of the *Journal of Discourses*, where the early sermons of the Mormon church were recorded. She read with amazement Brigham Young's teachings that the Civil War would never free the slaves, and that Mormons would never give up polygamy for statehood. But her distress deepened when she continued to read her great-great grandfather's teachings that Adam had been God, and then the teachings on "blood atonement," a Mormon doctrine that teaches that some sins are so serious that Christ's blood cannot atone for them—that the sinner must himself have his own blood shed in order to obtain forgiveness. Most shocking of all to Sandra was learning that her ancestor had taught that it was the responsibility of a Mormon to cut the throat of someone whom he knew had committed a sin, such as adultery, that merited blood atonement.

Through all this reading, Sandra realized the struggle that her own mother, immersed in those scattered papers and history books, had waged for so many years. Sandra listened intently as Jerald shared passages from the *Book of Mormon* and from Isaiah with her which showed that there was only one God, and that he had existed from eternity. He showed her verses in the Bible that she had never seen—verses that told about true salvation and eternal life.

"Through all this," Sandra remembers, "I gave up Mormonism." But she was not willing at that time to make the same commitment to Jesus Christ that Jerald had made. She had stayed at her grandmother's house since meeting Jerald, and when, after a few weeks, he asked her to marry him, their whirlwind courtship concluded with their marriage two months later at her parents' home in California.

Jerald took Sandra to many different churches in the San Fernando Valley and Burbank areas, hoping that she would be touched by some minister's sermon and make the decision to dedicate her life to Christ. But it wasn't until October 24, 1959, when she heard a radio preacher's sermon on First John 4:10: "Herein is love, not that we loved God, but that he loved us, and sent his Son to be the propitiation for our sins" that she made a commitment to that Son. She later asked for and received Christian baptism.

For two years she and Jerald lived out that commitment while still believing the *Book of Mormon* to be a second witness for Christ. It was not until they turned the same critical attention to the *Book of Mormon* that they had given to the other Mormon teachings that they realized that it, too, was false.

8

Latayne C. Scott

I was about thirteen when I went before Garland F. Bushman, the patriarch of the stake, or area, in which I lived. Patriarch Bushman placed his hands on my head and said, "In the preexistence, you were one of the choice souls of heaven noted by Father Abraham. Your ancestors were noble people, of the tribe of Ephraim. You yourself have a great destiny—to become a leader of women in the church and in the state where you will reside. You will meet a fine young man, be married in a temple of our Lord, and raise up righteous children. Finally, you will arise in the morning of the first resurrection, surrounded by your family."

These wonderful predictions made me weep for joy. The patriarch warned me, however, that Satan wanted my soul very much—so much, in fact, that he would try hard to deceive me. All the blessings promised me would therefore be conditional upon my resisting Satan, and my obedience to the precepts of Mormonism.

It wasn't easy to leave. I owed, and still owe, the Mormon church and its members a great debt of gratitude. But I am regarded by them as a traitor and an apostate. I left Mormonism after tasting some of its sweetest fruits.

Through the tumultuous years of adolescence—those years of being too tall, too clumsy, and having pimples and glasses—the Mormon church was security. Teachers and counselors in the church were compassionate and truly interested in me.- These people were bound together by great love for their families (how rare in this day!), the church, and each other.

The excellent youth programs (including track meets, road shows, supervised dances, cookouts, camps, sports activities, firesides, work and service projects, and much more) filled a gap in my life that might otherwise have been filled with early dating and associations in unsavory places. Through Mormonism I found a concrete way to express my fervent love for God and my desires to serve him. I gave love freely, and had it returned one hundredfold.

Some of Mormonism's blessings were even more tangible. I received an education of the highest quality at Brigham Young University (BYU), and through writing contests I was awarded scholarships that made it easier for me to attend. The part-time jobs I held while in school (dorm resident assistant, staff writer for the university's weekly magazines, translation and public relations work for the Latin-American Studies Department, and counter work at the basketball arena's concessions stand) were provided by the BYU board of trustees, who were deeply interested in the welfare of its students.

Once even the food I ate was provided by the Mormon church. My father had undergone extensive surgery, and when the church officials heard of this, they brought hot meals to our home for several days and assessed our grocery supply to determine what we needed. They returned with sacks and sacks of staple grocery items, and even offered to make car, house, and utility payments if needed.

I loved Mormonism for these things, and returned my love by living and serving as a "good Mormon." Each time that I was interviewed by my bishop and asked about such things as my attendance at meetings, my payment of tithing, observance of the Word of Wisdom (health laws), sexual purity, and support of church doctrines and leaders,

I was awarded a coveted "temple recommend" which allowed me as a faithful member to enter any Mormon temple to participate in sacred ordinances there.

During my young adulthood, I served as a teacher in Sunday School, Relief Society (ladies' organization), and in Primary (children's organization). I was active as a speaker in Sacrament meetings and was often called on to prepare programs for MIA (youth organization) and for special occasions. For a while I worked as my ward's (congregation's) media aids supervisor, and in various other church "jobs."

I was never lukewarm. I lived Mormonism; I loved it—and I left it.

My "apostasy" did not happen overnight. Once the process began, however, it moved quickly. When I returned to my home in Albuquerque, New Mexico, for summer vacation in 1973, my plans were set. I would work at the International Airport, earn the money that along with a partial scholarship for poetry, would pay for my fourth and final year at BYU. I had begun the process of revising *El Gaucho*, a Spanish textbook written by Sid Shreeve, the head of BYU's Latin-American Studies department. I regarded the summer away from BYU as a necessary evil, and I was anxious to return to that Mormon microcosm.

I was annoyed when my mother, who played ragtime piano at a local pizza parlor, suggested that I date non-Mormons that summer. A missionary I was "waiting for" was due to return that fall, and I just wasn't interested. Besides, I was kept busy between my summer job and the book revision. One night, though, when I went to pick Mother up at work, she introduced me to a young man she had described in glowing terms (which had fallen on disinterested ears).

Dan Scott, the object of her praises, started off our introductory conversation by saying, "So, you're a Mormon. I've read the *Book of Mormon*. It was, uh, interesting." Immediately I thought to myself, *Maybe he could be converted.*

Then, more cautious, I stalled, searching for a reply. Everyone I'd ever known who'd read the whole *Book of Mormon* had been converted to the Mormon church. In fact, I reflected, I'd known plenty of "faithful" Mormons who had never read the whole book unless and until required to do so in a religion class or while on a mission. *Perhaps,* I thought, *this would be a good time to terminate our discussion,* and I left quickly.

A few weeks later, a voice on the phone said, "Hi! Bet you don't know who this is!" His Tennessee accent had betrayed him. I said, "Yes—Dan Scott." He was crushed, his surprise foiled, but not crushed enough not to ask me out. I accepted against my better judgment.

Our first date was a disaster. He took me out to mid-week services at his church where he announced, "She's a Mormon." I was stared at as if I were from another planet. Nonetheless, I was attracted by Dan's openness and decided to date him again if he asked, and he did. I soon found Dan to be a true and warm friend with a sense of humor he could aim at himself as well as at others.

Our only disagreements came when we discussed religion. He was so transparently shocked when I answered his questions about baptism for the dead, polygamy, and Negroes and the Mormon priesthood that we made an agreement. He would study the *Book of Mormon* and other Mormon scripture with me if I would study the Bible with him. I felt this to be a personal triumph, because I'd never studied Mormonism with anyone (except my mother) who did not join the Mormon church.

Soon Dan and I had to admit to ourselves the love that was growing between us. One thing we both agreed on: We could not take the chance of becoming more deeply involved with our hearts so near and our souls so far apart. Our discussions usually put me on the defensive. I was knowledgeable about my religion, and what was more, I was stubborn. Add to that a strong dose of love for the doctrines and people of Mormonism, and you have an idea of the battle Dan had to fight. He didn't fight it alone, though; he had several powerful weapons.

One was his brother-in-law, Charles Williamson, a preacher of great intelligence and patience. One day Charles and I agreed to sit down and talk only about religion. We sat on opposite sides of a table, me with my Bible, *Book of Mormon, Doctrine and Covenants, Pearl of Great Price,* and *Principles of the Gospel*; he with his Bible. Dan soon left the room, a scene he described as a "verbal Ping-Pong game." Both Charles and I were exhausted after about two hours of table-slamming debate. I was on the verge of anger. I learned later that Charles told Dan in confidence that I knew more than any Mormon elder he'd ever spoken with, and frankly he didn't know if there was any hope for me.

My recurring headaches signaled tension that had begun to grow as my doubts had. Dan and Charles didn't think their talks had served any purpose. I was filled with a sick dread that I then thought was a godly sorrow for the lost souls of people like Dan and Charles. Actually, I was beginning to fear that my soul might be lost, and I dared not voice this fear—not even to myself.

Another of the mighty weapons used by Dan in the battle for my soul was the literature he somehow managed to find. These books dealt objectively and factually with Mormonism, from the view of non-Mormons. I was lucky that Dan chose the books he did for me to read. Most anti-Mormon literature I had previously read had had very little effect on me.

The most effective weapon of all in Dan's armory was three-pronged. First was his overwhelming faith and confidence in the Word of God, the Bible. Second was the prayer that he continually offered for my soul's enlightenment. Third, (and most penetrating) was the love he had for me. Had we not loved each other, I don't believe I would have had the courage to leave the comfortable Mormon way of life. Had he ceased loving me before my conversion was completed, I fear I would have returned to the womb of Mormonism and lived there ever an infant, frightened and dependent, but secure in my deliberate ignorance.

I finally came to an impasse in my spiritual progress. I was struggling against the bonds of Mormonism—tradition and heritage, doctrinal comfort, and love. Yet I felt that something was terribly wrong there—why did my teachings and background in Mormonism conflict so sharply with my new knowledge of the Bible? Why the inconsistencies in LDS historical accounts and early documents?

One final acid test remained at the end of the summer. Since I had a scholarship and a writing job waiting for me at BYU, I decided to return, promising Dan that we would marry—if I came back in December feeling about Mormonism as I did then in August. As I was packing, I felt as if the summer had been a dream. Or was it the real part, and the rest of my past life the illusion? I was unhappy about leaving Dan, but I knew I must make my decision alone. No matter how much I loved him, my eternal soul—and my relationship with God—was more important to me.

I was putting my books into boxes when, tired, I sat down with my *Doctrine and Covenants.* Always it had been my favorite book of scripture because of its practical commandments, like the Word of Wisdom, which had purified and uplifted the lives of millions of Mormons. Also commonly bound in the same volume with the *Doctrine and Covenants* is another book of scripture called the *Pearl of Great Price,* which includes two books the Mormons believe were written by Moses and Abraham. These scriptures are unique in that they have what purport to be illustrations by Abraham himself. These illustrations, reproduced by woodcuts, are in the ancient Egyptian style. I have always loved Egyptology, though I have no more than an avid layperson's knowledge of the subject.

I was looking idly through these familiar woodcuts when I was struck by an incongruity that upset me. Two of the women had been labeled in the woodcut by Joseph Smith as men! Egyptian women are easily identified in ancient documents by their distinctive strapped, ankle-length dresses.

Why I had never noticed this before, I do not know. I had studied and read about these woodcuts for years. I knew from reading standard authorities on Egyptology that Egyptian women in history had dressed as men and acted as Pharaoh (Queen Hatshepsut, for example) but no Egyptian man would have been caught dead in a woman's clothing, especially to be preserved for posterity on a papyrus roll!

It was with this discovery that my most concrete doubts about Mormonism began to multiply. No anti-Mormon writer had pointed this out; no hater of the LDS church could have falsified or altered these prints; they were in my own personal copy of scripture. I found myself crushed and exultant, all at the same time.

When I arrived in Provo, I set about making myself as busy as possible. Soon old friends began to arrive for the school year, and I fooled myself by thinking they wouldn't notice the difference in me. I registered for classes, reported for work, and caught up on all the news of who had married whom, who had gone on missions, and whose missionaries had returned.

But I have never been a good deceiver, and soon my feelings about the church began to surface. Close friends made no secret of the fact that they thought I'd gone crazy. Some attributed my change of heart to a broken relationship with a missionary. Many of my Mormon friends, to this day, assume that I wanted to leave Mormonism because of that missionary. An unhappy bargain that would be—to trade my soul's salvation for revenge!

I became even more upset each time I attended church services. Nothing had changed as much as I had, and I was sick at heart. Late one afternoon I was asked to meet with my branch president. Newly appointed to this job, he was nervous and unsure of himself. Everyone in his BYU student branch was to be interviewed and assigned a church job—teaching, visitation, social activity planning—and he seemed anxious to get these assignments over.

He began by congratulating me on my past service in

the church (he had my records before him), then asked a question he thought would put us on common ground.

"Well, Latayne," he said, leaning back in his chair, "how do you feel about the Prophet?"

Just that week, Harold B. Lee, the "Prophet, Seer and Revelator of the Church," had come to BYU. When I had seen twenty-five thousand students rise to their feet and sing through tear-choked throats the song "We Thank Thee, Oh, God, for a Prophet," I had felt faint and ill. How could I now tell this branch president of my feelings?

I looked away and said, "I don't think he is a prophet."

The young president sat up so suddenly that the back of his chair snapped forward. He acted as if he had had a bad day, and I was pulling a very, very poor joke on him. I tried to explain that I hadn't come to a decision about the church, that I wanted to avoid talking about it publicly, but still wanted to attend services and work in the church.

He only shook his head, his disbelief turning to anger. "How can you think such things?" he asked. "Don't you know that if you leave the church you'll never be able to reach the Celestial Kingdom? You will never be happy again!"

Never to be happy again! What a load to put upon a young mind already troubled with uncertainty and fear of displeasing God! I left that interview with dread in my soul. I went back to my apartment. That night I called Dan, and the next day disenrolled from Brigham Young University, telling only a few of my decision. My roommates were incredulous, my landlady tearful and reproachful, and all but one school official unsympathetic. A similar conflict, this registrar told me, had faced him when he was young. He had taken the part of Mormonism with few regrets, but his experience made him understanding and concerned with my best interests.

When I arrived back in Albuquerque, little of the pressure was relieved. I received many letters, most anonymous and many cruel, which persuaded and threatened, pleaded and rejected. All had one object in mind—my return to Mormonism. Many pleaded, saying that my leaving would affect those I had taught and helped to convert, or those weak in the faith. (I pray to God it may be so!) Some of the letters told of the punishments awaiting apostates, and one ended by saying, "Don't you realize that you'll *never* see the inside of a temple again?"

Phone calls, too, didn't diminish for several months. Most were from friends who had "heard and just couldn't believe it." Close friends called one night and said that several dozen other friends would be fasting and praying together the next day for me. On that day, I, too, fasted and prayed for my soul, for though I felt that I should leave Mormonism, I wasn't sure that Dan's teachings were any more reliable. Once you've found the tenets you most trusted and believed in to be false, you're not anxious to embrace a substitute.

Of only one thing was I certain: however I might begin to comprehend God, I knew that he loved me and knew my anguish, and would show me the way through his Son. This, and no more, could I be sure of.

Even Dan, much as I loved him, could not be the basis of my faith. I knew that if a group of people as dedicated and as sincere as most Mormons could be so wrong, then so could Dan and his teachings. I have never felt more alone in my life.

I labored in agony with the great questions that left me sick at heart and spiritually weakened. I pulled this burden along behind me, pushed it before me, and tried to take it upon my shoulders. When I found that I could not move it alone—it was too heavy—I gave up and did what I should have done long before. I put it in God's hands, and wondered why I had taken so long to make that wisest of decisions in my life.

I spent a lot of time reading everything I could get my hands on that dealt objectively with Mormonism. I was fascinated and repelled the more I realized my errors. A near-physical sickness would engulf me when I stopped to realize how I had flirted with hell while thinking I was courting heaven.

I realized how it is that any religious group teaching false doctrine can so easily misinterpret the Scriptures to someone who is unfamiliar with them. The greatest battles a cult can wage over the soul of the ignorant man, I believe, are already won when the proselyte is too lazy, or afraid, or unwilling to seek a more correct interpretation of a Scripture passage that teaches a "new" doctrine. We have nothing to fear but ourselves when we ignore the admonition to "search the Scriptures."

I had realized this too late to undo my years in Mormonism. I cannot say that I wish I had never been a Mormon. God richly blessed me during those years. Perhaps they were a preparation for my Christian life. I do not question or doubt the wisdom of God, even though I still sorrow for the wrong things I did and taught.

I knew then as now that I must recommit myself to God—I must become a new creature, as different from my Mormon self as a butterfly from a caterpillar. I had so many doubts—not knowing for certain what to trust or what doctrine was true. I decided on a course of action that included two things: I would be baptized for the remission of my many sins, and I would depend wholly on the Bible as my spiritual guide.

Dan was a little apprehensive as we prepared for my baptism. He was anxious and happy to baptize me, as I had requested. But he was afraid because he'd never baptized anyone before, and he feared he would let me slip into the water or choke. I could only laugh—I knew I could take care of myself in that situation, because I once had been baptized thirty consecutive times (all within a matter of minutes) while doing ordinances for the dead in the Manti, Utah, Mormon temple!

The baptism by Dan was different though. That still September night, I felt a great sense of the majesty of God, and his mercy so undeserved by me, a sinner. Once I realized that God had forgiven and forgotten my sins, I was able to forgive myself and begin trusting him for guidance.

I feel a debt to Mormonism. Mormons may regard a book showing the errors of Mormonism a strange way to repay a debt of gratitude. I only wish that when I was a Mormon someone had told me the things of which I write.

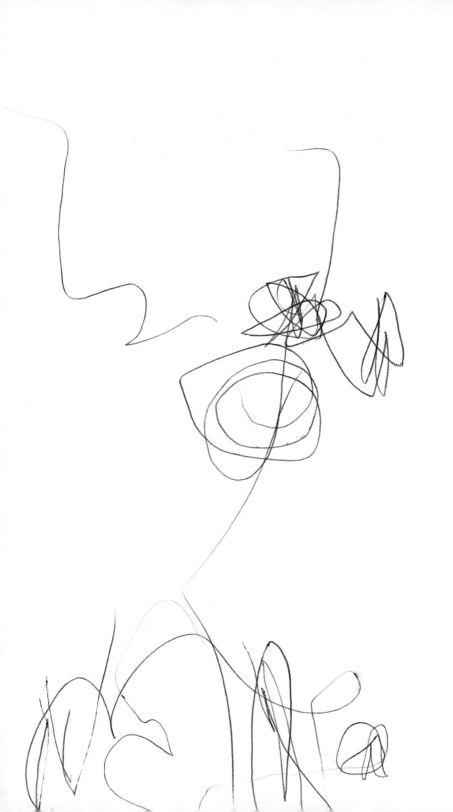

PART TWO

Identifying Factors Involved in Leaving Mormonism and Effective Nurture of Ex-Mormons

9

Personal Costs and Compensations

At what personal cost did you leave Mormonism?

What effect did this have on family and friends?

What seemed to compensate for these costs to yourself and to others?

Randy Steele

The most obvious cost, of course, was my family. I had a happy family life before, and now I am very far away from them in a lot of ways.

I believe if you remain faithful to the Lord, obey him, and live the gospel for him, he will bless you for it.

I believe he will fight your battles for you. This I learned the hard way, because I started out fighting my own battles when my family didn't come out of Mormonism with me. Now they still haven't come out, but the Lord has been with me and has strengthened me, and given me comfort in my life, for I have no fears about tomorrow.

Dave Wilkins

As far as what I regard as personal cost, I believe it was very light for me. I haven't felt much personal loss. I have felt tremendous personal freedom especially from a hierarchical structure.

Since my family did not really know how I was feeling when I was in the process of leaving the Mormon church, they didn't really oppose it. My mother would send my address to church officials in whatever town I lived, so that they would send home teachers to my house but this had little effect on me.

My relationship with my family has basically remained intact. My mother is very unhappy with my decision and tells me so, but she knows my decision is final. I have gotten different reactions from my brothers, however. One brother actually refused to listen to my reasons for leaving—he put his hands over his ears. Another brother, though, has shared with me his frustration over the "politics" in Mormonism—the hierarchy and rules and changes in rules bother him just as they did me.

I was excommunicated from the Mormon church at my own request, almost ten years after I made the decision to become a Christian. For the first six years of that time, I continued to have contact with missionaries and home teachers. I hope that I have had some success in raising some doubts in their minds about Mormon theology.

All in all the cost of leaving Mormonism has not been much compared with the compensation of knowing Christ and the freedom he allows. There's not much that I feel I left.

Cindy Bauer

One immediate effect of my declaration of wanting to live for Jesus Christ was that my mother, my only parent, asked me to leave home, because she did not want me to influence my younger brother. My seminary students were called, and all my friends and peers were told to stay away from me.

People boycotted my wedding—they were called and told to stay away. But I have conscientiously tried to maintain contact with many of these friends, and show them that I still love them.

My brother (the one that my mother was concerned about), did eventually leave the Mormon church and have a real experience with the Lord Jesus. At my mother's funeral, however, my uncle who had baptized me into the Mormon church told me that I had deeply hurt and embarrassed my mother by my actions. Of course that was devastating to me, but I had to keep in mind the reason for my actions: Jesus.

Some things that had been very important to me lost their value. I had food stored, as I had been commanded by my Mormon leaders (hundreds of pounds of wheat and a grinder, for instance), that I ended up selling at a fraction of its value. And then there was my collection of Mormon books!

But God has more than compensated. What Mormon friends I lost have been replaced by Christian friends. And my study of Mormonism has made those books valuable to me in a way that they never were before.

Once I accepted Jesus, I have not had any regrets. The joy of knowing him for the first minute has more than made up for anything I ever lost in leaving the Mormon church.

Sheila Garrigus

When I left the Mormon church, I lost all of my Mormon friends. None of them would talk to me. If I met them in public (at the grocery store, or at the mall), I would speak to them but they would turn and walk away without acknowledging my greeting. This hurt so badly. I had new Christian friends who were very dear, but it was years before I had anyone who could take the place of Paula Anderson, who was my dearest friend in the whole world. It wasn't until I met other ex-Mormons who had come to the Lord, people who became my strongest support base, that I again felt deep friendship. We all have the same background, we all bought the same lie, and we all know how precious Mormons are as individuals and as a people

I have known others who have left Mormonism and lost everything—family, jobs, *everything*. I was very fortunate because I did not lose my family when I came out of the Mormon church—if anything, I lost them when I became a Mormon.

Granny Geer

The day I was baptized, none of my Mormon relatives would come to church to share that with me. With the joy I was feeling over my salvation, their reaction almost broke my heart. But later, when I was sharing my sadness with my Uncle Tom, he said to me, "Well, honey, why didn't you ask me? I would have been glad to come!" He continued to listen as I witnessed to him, and as a result became a Christian—the first person I was able to bring to the Lord!

It took twenty-six years of repeated witnessing, though, to bring my beloved mother to trust the Lord for full salvation. I regret those years of lost fellowship with her; the hours we could have spent together, rejoicing over our salvation instead of the heartache-filled times with each of us believing the other was eternally lost. It was not until the closing hours of her life that my dear mother finally accepted the Lord as her only Savior as I tenderly sang to her "Whispering Hope."

I know I will meet my precious Mama in eternity. However, I remember how horrifying the experience was when, as a three-week-old Christian, I realized that my dear father will have to spend eternity in a very real hell that the Scripture (2 Thess 1:19) clearly says is not temporary.

It still burdens my heart to meet Mormons who are in the same position my daddy was in, who believe that they'll get a second chance to atone personally for their own negligence and sins; and who believe that they cannot go to the highest heaven without the consent of Joseph Smith. I don't want anyone else to die full of such false hopes and without Jesus, like my daddy did.

Kevin Bond

When we left the church, we resigned from it. We did not want the stigma of excommunication, and all that means to the Mormon mind, hanging over us. We still wanted to be regarded as part of the community because Mormons were still our neighbors and friends. At the time we left, there was a great flood disaster, and we made it very clear to the stake president that we wanted to be included in service to the community.

Our Mormon friends have been, for the most part, supportive once they realized our decision was final. Some have commented on our courage and on the change they have seen in me. Of course I no longer have the "common ground" with them that the church once provided but also few hard feelings.

The real cost to me involved family. Michelle's family as well as my own have had a lot of trouble accepting our decision. My father took it hardest of all—he treated it like a divorce in the family. Our lines of communication have always remained open, but at first they were very narrow and diplomatic. They have widened with the years and the love that my father and I have for each other, in spite of religion, is our point of contact.

There have also been times of spiritual testing that followed our "honeymoon" of being new Christians. But none of these things can dim the joy I have in the saving knowledge of Jesus Christ, and the hope I have in his return and the coming glory.

Sandra Tanner

I don't think I could have made it through that difficult time if I hadn't had Jerald standing by me. Many times when I visited with family members, I would come home in tears. My first year as a Christian was a joyous time to be a child of God, but it was a heartbreaking time as far as my family was concerned. Every encounter put pressure on me to conform, to come back to the fold.

My relatives would ask me, "Why do you want to make waves by distributing pamphlets that make the church look bad? How can a young person like you find answers that older people haven't? Do you think that our whole family has been wrong all these years? Did your great-grandparents come across the plains for nothing? How can you turn your back on the sacrifices they made? Are you trying to make fun of them?"

We finally decided to leave California and move to Salt Lake City. Though there were not as many of my close relatives there, it had its own set of problems, as you can imagine.

Latayne Scott

At the time that I began to critically investigate the doctrines of Mormonism, my entire life was centered around the Mormon church, and all my close friends were Mormons. I had discussed with my bishop the possibility of serving a two-year, full-time mission for the church.

I had a small silver charm of the Salt Lake Temple that I wore around my neck constantly, and it signified my great dream of being married there. (Even after I left Mormonism, the lure of eternal marriage was strong, and when I wrote my wedding vows for my marriage to Dan, I intended that this union be for eternity, because I was not willing to give up the doctrine of eternal marriage.)

To me the greatest cost of leaving Mormonism was that it shattered all the dreams that I had built my life around. Even though I knew that I had made the right decision in leaving Mormonism, it was truly an act of submission to a God I knew I could not fight.

I knew that he had forgiven my sins. I knew that he loved me. But it was years before I could bring myself to trust God, because the last god I had trusted and built my life around was only an illusion.

It took a long time before I could wholeheartedly love God and seek intimacy with him. In this aspect of my life, though, he has more than compensated for "the years the locusts hath eaten" (Joel 2:25). I can truly say he is the most influential and essential personality in my life, and I treasure my closeness with him.

10

Opposition from the Mormon Church

What techniques were used by Mormon friends and family and church officials to prevent and/or oppose your decision to leave Mormonism?

Randy Steele

The techniques fell into three categories: my wife's emotional response to my doubts; the actions of local and church-wide officials in trying to persuade me to stay in the church; and the involvement of people like the Browns who pictured people who leave Mormonism as unstable and sometimes immoral.

Cindy Bauer

I don't believe anyone in the Mormon church really thought I would ever leave (I never would have believed it myself), so no one tried to prevent me from leaving before I actually did. During the time of my decision, I kept my searching to myself, because I didn't want on the one hand to lose face with Mormons, nor to let Christians know that they were reaching me.

But once word got out that I did leave, some people in

church really moved fast. Before I left for Israel, I was put on a plane with my Mormon friend Della to go and talk to the General Authorities of the church in Salt Lake City. In Utah that day, I met three different officials of the church, and obtained each one's permission to tape record our conversations.

The first man I talked to was the Church Historian, who talked to me about fallacies connected with the Book of Abraham. I don't remember what he said, exactly, except for the fact that it seemed like he was fishing for things.

Next I met with Brother Mortizson, a writer of church curriculums for Seminary and Institute programs. He had been a personal hero of mine, and I had learned much from him. He greeted me very warmly until he found the reason for my visit. Then he said, "Well, Satan has you by the neck."

Della and I went from his office to that of Neal Maxwell, a prominent General Authority. He listened to what I had to say and commented, "Well, I can see that you have had a real experience with Jesus." He left me with a final challenge: holding the *Book of Mormon* in his hand, he told me that I would have to give up the sacred writings should I follow through with my decision.

When someone leaves the Mormon church, people assume that it is for one of three reasons. The first is the assumption that *you never really had a testimony to begin with.* Of course the many students I taught would not be able to say that.

The second reason would be because of *sin or the desire to sin.* One friend actually called me and told me that the reason I left the church was so that I could drink. I have never drunk alcohol, nor tasted even coffee or tea. To this day, I live the Word of Wisdom more completely than most Mormons because I do not use caffeine in any form, and I limit my intake of meat, which is a commandment also found in the Word of Wisdom passage. Nor did I leave the church to sin sexually, which was another possibility this caller hinted at.

The third reason people think that someone might leave Mormonism is *because of personal problems with someone in the ward.* My friend Della was accused by her Mormon brothers and sisters of having hurt me in some way; to such an extent, in fact, that she felt tremendous guilt. She made an appointment to speak to me and find out what she had done wrong. I put my arms around her and assured her that I was leaving because of Jesus, not because of anything she had done to me.

Most of my relatives had little to say about my leaving except my uncle, the high priest.

Sheila Garrigus

My bishop gave me three options, which included the option to divorce Jim. Also in that conversation my bishop told me that as my spiritual advisor, he counseled me to (1) stop going to Bible studies; and (2) stop reading just the Bible; and (3) if I wanted reading material to go to the LDS bookstore and get Mormon literature there.

Once I had decided to leave Mormonism, my home teacher spent a lot of time trying to lovingly talk me out of it. I also got many phone calls from friends who were hurt by the news they'd heard, and would ask, "Have I done anything?" "What can we do?" "Has someone hurt your feelings?" "Please don't take this drastic step."

The most effective influence that kept me in the Mormon church, though, was not an earthly person. It was the experience that I had of seeing what I thought was my grandmother. I believe that what I saw was a familiar spirit, a demonic spirit that wanted me to believe I was seeing my Grandmother McInnes to deceive me. That deception kept me in years of spiritual bondage and oppression.

Granny Geer

As soon as my mother knew that I was attending the Baptist church, she began to prevail on me to read books she had on Mormonism. But the Lord used those books to help me see the truth about Mormonism. For instance, the sermons at the Baptist church were centered around the virgin birth of Jesus, and when my mother insisted that I read the LDS book *Jesus the Christ* by James Talmadge, I learned for the first time in my thirty-one years as a Mormon that my church clearly taught contrary to the virgin birth.

She also had me read her adult Sunday School book, *The Vision*, and that's where I read the quote (pp. 59-60) from Brigham Young that states that no one will enter the Celestial Kingdom of God without the consent of Joseph Smith (*Journal of Discourses*, vol. 7, p. 289). When I heard the sermon the next week in the Baptist church on the pre-eminence of Jesus Christ, I was able to break away from that error I had been so long taught. But when I went to my mother that first Sunday afternoon in January and shared with her that I knew that Jesus Christ had died on the cross for my sins, and that I had that morning received him as my Savior, and now he lived in me, she begged me never to go back to that church.

She also told me that I was in danger of breaking our family circle that was supposed to be complete throughout eternity, and that my father was being tormented by my actions in the spirit prison.

"Honey," she said as her tears dropped down on my head as I knelt with my face resting on her worn apron, "the things that were good enough for your poor, dead daddy and for me ought to be good enough for you."

Even after I began traveling and speaking—"pioneering for the *real* Jesus"—my mother would follow me all the way to the bus station, pleading, "Honey, be a good girl, and don't go talk about the Mormons."

My sister also came to me and told me how my actions would hurt her little daughter, Bobbie Jayne, who had been dead ten years and who had been like a sister to my daughter Jacqueline. "I don't care that you have left the Mormon church and are going to hell," my sister sobbed, "but why must you take your little daughter along? Now Bobbie Jayne is in heaven weeping, because she will never get to be with your little Jackie again!" According to Mormon doctrine, Bobby Jayne would be eternally disadvantaged and grieved. Supposedly she and Papa were waiting in the LDS intermediate "spirit-place" for me and Jackie to join them.

Nevertheless I went about my little farming community to my uncles and aunts and cousins and people I'd known all my life. I wanted them to know how happy I was to belong to the Lord Jesus Christ. I was amazed at the love I felt for them, but I found that they no longer loved me. They spurned my efforts to talk with them, caustically rebuked me, and censured me for causing Mama so much grief. They made fun of me, telling me how tiresome it would be in my heaven, sitting on a cloud, strumming a harp and singing about Jesus.

Finally one day my bishop repeated that again to me, and I told him, "But, sir, what you anticipate doing in your heaven will be much, much more tiresome. You're going to be having babies all through eternity. That's a lot more tiresome than singing, serving and praising the Lord forever!"

Kevin Bond

When we left the church Michelle was Relief Society homemaking teacher, and I was our elders' quorum instructor.

Just after I taught my last elder's quorum lesson—exclusively out of the Bible, I might add—I had the elders quorum presidency sit down with me so that I could tell them that I had decided to leave the church. Some of them were in tears.

One man told me, "I don't understand why you are leaving, and I don't think I care. I haven't read the Old Testament. I don't care to. I have the *Book of Mormon*. I don't think I need to be scholarly or to find anything else out."

I told them that my main reason for leaving was that I could not reconcile Mormonism to the first-century church of the New Testament, but this did not seem to have much effect on them.

The process of getting our resignation accepted was very long and drawn-out. I know this is done so that people can have a chance to reconsider, but it was very taxing on us.

My parents have told me that they think that I left the church so that I could drink. I have tried to explain to them that that is like coming upon the scene of an automobile accident where the police have checked everything out and concluded that since they could find no other cause, perhaps the driver was swatting at a bee and lost control of the car. To extend the analogy to my leaving Mormonism: I didn't leave the car of Mormonism because of annoyance—the whole structure was consumed with flames, and I jumped out to save my life.

My mother, too, has persistently and lovingly tried to get me to reconsider. But I have reminded my parents of the other point of view I have, which is that they, by leaving their fundamentalist Christian backgrounds for Mormonism, are really the ones who have apostatized. I have merely returned.

One LDS man who has been a faithful friend believes that we have not left permanently; or if we have, that we were taken outside the church by God to do some special work, but that we will still be in the Celestial Kingdom.

But my older brother, Steve (who also left the church), and I do not believe that. We believe that we have burst the bonds of Mormonism and run straight into the arms of the Lord.

Sandra Tanner

Jerald and I tried to talk to our Mormon families about why we didn't believe in Mormonism anymore. My father's attitude was that this was just a symptom of youth, that I would with maturity encounter life's trials and problems that would reveal that Christianity was just a useless utopian concept, and that I would at that time come to my senses and return to Mormonism.

My mother, who had in a way started my whole route

out of the church, did not want me to leave it for two reasons: she valued the closeness of Mormon society, and she feared that my leaving it would alienate me from the rest of the family.

One day one of my aunts came to my home. "You are driving your mother insane," she said. "She is going to have a nervous breakdown over this. Don't you talk to me about the love of God—any girl who was a Christian would never hurt someone she loved this way. Christ would want you to come back to the church and be part of your family again."

When I explained that this was not an issue of people's feeling, but of my eternal destiny, she seemed unmoved. But she did call me back a few weeks later and tell me that she had seen my sincerity, and knew that I had to follow my conscience.

Another aunt was a little more blunt. The first Christmas Jerald and I were married she sent us a Christmas card—the "Peace on earth" variety—with a hand-written note that included a *Book of Mormon* verse. It said, "If thou wilt of thyself be destroyed, seek no more to destroy the church of God" [Alma 36:9]. "Merry Christmas. Love . . ." and her name.

After we wrote a letter about our Christian commitment to Jerald's older sister, a devout Mormon, she and her husband wrote us and asked us if we would be willing to fast and pray to see if Mormonism were true. We wrote back that we would be happy to do so if they would agree to fast and pray to see if it were not true. They refused this idea.

The truth is that while others of our family had left to become members of non-Christian groups, it did not have the effect that our becoming Christians did. They saw Christianity as too narrow-minded, a fanatic sect. We were not even speaking the same language. When I would tell them that I was a Christian and was now saved they would ask me, "Saved from what?"

I did talk to my bishop about some of the things I was

reading when I first started studying with Jerald. But he assumed that I was following Jerald, that I hadn't really thought things out for myself. I asked the bishop some of the questions that were particularly troubling to me, and he referred me to a man in our ward whom he said had done some intensive study and could answer them for me. I was very disappointed when this man told me to read *Doctrines of Salvation* and *Answers to Gospel Questions*—two books that didn't even begin to penetrate to the depth of my own research.

The conclusion of the bishop and this man was that I had a rebellious attitude. If I had a teachable attitude, they reasoned, I should be able to go home and pray about it and receive the answers I needed to become a good, obedient Mormon.

Latayne Scott

I've already mentioned the reactions of the people at BYU when I shared with them my decision to leave the church. That was to be expected, I guess.

But what I didn't expect was the fact that no one in Albuquerque, my hometown, tried to talk to me about that decision once I returned. In fact I was a faithful, active member of the Church of Christ in Albuquerque for six years before I was excommunicated—and that at my own request.

It was actually very difficult to be excommunicated. I tried to start the procedure several months before *The Mormon Mirage* was published. My letter to my former bishop was never answered. The letter I sent to the stake center where he was stake president was returned because there was no mail box at the building. Finally I wrote a letter to the president of the Mormon Church in Salt Lake City, saying that if they did not honor my request to have my name removed that I would put a public notice in the newspaper.

A few days later I got a call from the bishop of the area in which I was then residing. He asked me some questions about why I wanted to take this course of action, and promised to call me back.

When he did call me back a few days later, he told me that they could not find any record of the fact that I had ever been a member of the Mormon church!

"You wouldn't happen to have any of your records, like your baptismal certificate, would you?" he asked. He seemed crestfallen when I answered that I did, and gave him the names of the two Mormon elders who baptized and confirmed me when I was eleven years old.

I learned later that a Mormon by the name of Steven L. Mayfield had, according to research done by the Tanners ("Statement on Mormon Spies,"[Salt Lake City: Modern Microfilm, July 22, 1980]) prepared an "enemies list" that included my name, and that under the alias of Stan Fields had corresponded with me about the book I was writing, *The Mormon Mirage.* My guess is that the LDS church officials sought to blunt the effectiveness of this forthcoming book by claiming that I had never been a Mormon at all. (Now that I realize the importance of the documentation of my membership in the Mormon church, I keep it in a safe deposit box.)

I was excommunicated at my own request from the LDS Church on December 20, 1979, on the grounds of apostasy.

11

Mistakes Christians Make

What mistakes did Christians make in trying to influence you for Christ?

Randy Steele

I haven't recalled any mistakes made by the Christians who witnessed to me.

When I was in the process of coming out of Mormonism, I wrote to a man who was a Mormon, who had considered leaving the church but had changed his mind. He told me that one of his reasons for staying in Mormonism was that the Christians who witnessed to him were aggressive and "hysterical." That, of course, was not my experience.

Dave Wilkins

When we were still living in Las Cruces, the Baptist church we were attending brought in a man who gave a presentation on Mormonism. I thought he was abrasive. I resented the fact that when he found out that I was a Mormon, he made a point of directing some of his comments at me. Then when his presentation was over he made a beeline to corner me.

But if you asked LaNell about that same incident, she would tell you that that man gave her a real "beacon of light." Here was someone who had the scriptural answers to the conflicts that were raging within her. She felt very much alone in her fight against Mormonism and was deeply grateful to this man.

I guess I would have to say that this preacher's approach was not helpful to me and yet very encouraging to LaNell.

About the only other "mistake" Christians made in dealing with us happened about five days before we left Denver. Our neighbors contacted us, and we agreed to let them bring over a man who tried to convert us and baptize us all in one night—hurry, hurry. It was just too rushed and overwhelming for us.

One mistake that Christians did not make in dealing with us was in telling us that we were wrong or going to hell. They chose to be our friends instead of our accusers.

Cindy Bauer

I can really, honestly think of none—I probably had one of the best witnessing experiences that anybody has ever had. But I have seen Christians make mistakes in witnessing to other Mormons. I have seen Christians approach a Mormon in pride, with a know-it-all attitude. This is such a contrast to the humble, loving attitudes portrayed by the people who witnessed so effectively to me.

I've seen Christians put Mormons down, speaking very curtly to them, implying that only an idiot would believe what they believe. Christians have to keep uppermost in their minds that Mormons are deeply deceived but not stupid. There are too many Mormon doctors and lawyers and national and state officials who are Mormons for anyone to think they are stupid. They are also most generally very sincere in what they believe. But again, sincerity doesn't always equal truth.

Sheila Garrigus

Pastor Jim in Illinois argued with me about Mormon doctrine when we first got married. That was harmful. I contrast that with the other pastor who talked with me. Though he was loving, he was so unacquainted with Mormon terminology—actually the misuse of Christian terminology—that we could not effectively communicate. But their love and concern for me came through loud and clear.

The greatest harm, though, was done by well-intentioned Christians who actually attacked the Mormon church and its doctrines in my presence. They were a great stumbling block for me, especially when they held my beliefs up to ridicule.

That did nothing but make me angry, and make me protective of the church. It made no difference in my mind at that point whether or not what they were saying was correct: I felt that they were attacking me as well as my church.

Granny Geer

I went thirty-one years of my life without hearing the truth about Jesus Christ. The mistake that Christians made with me was in not telling me what my soul needed to know. No one quoted John 3:16 to me.

The day after I was saved, I wrote a letter to a Baptist friend I had known all my life. I knew all along there was something different, something very special, about this woman, but I didn't know why until I was saved.

"I'm a Christian now, too," I wrote her. "And now I know what made you different. I want you to know that I, too, have invited Jesus to be my Savior."

In the next mail came a little, tear-stained letter from her. "Oh, honey, forgive me," it read, "forgive me for not telling you myself. I didn't want to hurt your mother and your father's feelings."

And my heart cried out, and still cries out: "Would to God that she had been willing to hurt my father's feelings, rather than letting him die and go to hell."

I am so grateful that my beloved Ernest and his family, especially Lonnie, Mamie Lou, and "Grandpa" Geer, helped me pass not only from death to life, but helped me also to sort out and discard nonbiblical LDS teachings. They, along with the Southern Baptist missionary T. T. Reynolds and his lovely wife, Nina, helped me learn to "cling to that which is good."

Kevin Bond

There was a Christian lady who announced to Michelle and me that she was "claiming" us for the Lord. It wasn't at all like Jane Tallant's persistent witnessing. This kind of struck me as being pretentious and pious, because we became her "project." I believe that if you want to "claim" someone for the Lord that should be between you and the Lord.

Once when I was trying to sort the facts out about Mormonism, I met an ex-Mormon man who agreed to talk to me. But instead of just answering my questions, he deluged me with information. I was so overwhelmed with the amount of information he gave me that it was really too much for me.

All in all, though, Christians have been patient and understanding with us. Though I believe that there is a time for being plainspoken, I think ex-Mormons really should be treated with kid gloves. There are just so many emotions involved.

Sandra Tanner

The biggest problem was that both before and after I left Mormonism, there were very few Christians who knew anything about Mormonism. We were lost out in this great sea of the Protestant world, with no one who understood how we felt, or who could point the way for us.

This was the case with the girl who told me that it was "blasphemy" to say that God was once a man—she knew it was wrong according to her understanding of Scripture, but she didn't tell me why it was wrong.

As a teenager I attended regularly one summer some interdenominational youth meetings that were held in homes in my neighborhood. It was great fun, and genuine fellowship, but no one ever directly talked to me about the difference between Mormonism and Christianity. Since no one addressed the issue—I was never challenged—there was nothing to resolve. Meanwhile I had a condescending attitude that I see still today in other Mormons who assume that Christians have "half the light" and who could be Super Christians only if they became Mormons.

Even after Jerald and I left Mormonism and began visiting Christian churches in our area, we found that most Christians had no idea of how to talk to us about what we had come out of, nor how to handle our situations with our families.

Meanwhile I was going through a major revamping of my thinking as I read the Bible. I found that the godly men of Genesis, for instance, were not practically perfect as I had been taught, but were humans with foibles just like me. I had to take a new look at the parables, at the Sermon on the Mount, at Paul's epistles, and ask myself, "What does it mean to be a Christian and not a Mormon?" This whole process would have been so much easier if we had had someone to help us.

There were two Mormon women that I met several years ago. They had never read any anti-Mormon literature but still they felt a spiritual longing and had decided to look outside Mormonism for its fulfillment. They came to our church, and it came up in class that they were still Mormons; and yet insisted that they were saved, that they had accepted Christ as their Savior. There was an ex-Mormon couple who were in the same class, and they pressed these two women to publicly acknowledge that Mormonism was wrong, and that they must be lost and they were going to hell. The two women had no reason at that point to feel "lost," and so they became so embarrassed with this public humiliation that they left the church. When I saw one of them some months later in the grocery store, she told me how sorrowful she was with her conclusion that the love she had so yearned for in

Mormonism didn't exist in Christianity either; that what she had found there was a group of people who were just as narrow-minded and condemning and impatient as Mormons. I tried to tell her that Christ's claims are far above the failings of men, and she agreed, up to a point. But the damage had been done: she had no desire to go to a Christian church again.

Jerald and I know some of the emotions that they felt, because we hung onto the *Book of Mormon* for two years after accepting Christ, and when some Christians who knew us at that point found this out, they more or less washed their hands of us, too.

Latayne Scott

I remember telling the pastor of the little Baptist church I'd attended that I'd become a Mormon. He stepped back from me as if I were diseased. Then he rubbed his hands together and muttered some thing about "false prophets" and "wolves in sheep's clothing" and walked away.

I don't mean to imply that he spoke harshly or unkindly. What hurts, in retrospect, is realizing that that was the last time I ever saw him. He never called me or tried to witness to me that he thought I had made a mistake, at a time when I was still impressionable. Perhaps he thought that losing one eleven-year old girl to Mormonism wasn't all that important.

My grandmother and cousin did try to talk to me about the fact that Mormonism encouraged me to "earn" my salvation, but they never sat down with a Bible and showed me what it had to say. I think I would have listened.

None of my other friends ever said anything to me about Mormonism except that they really admired their morals and lifestyle.

12

Toward an Easier Transition

What do you miss most about Mormonism?

What changes could individuals in the Christian body, as well as churches, institute that would make the transition to Christianity easier for an ex-Mormon?

What lacks do you see in Christianity as it is practiced now?

Randy Steele

Besides my family, I miss other elements of closeness that the Mormon church gives. I always looked forward to the social events, and remember especially the trips with other Mormons in a car to go to the temple. It was a time of special sharing and fellowship.

Because my family so strongly opposed my leaving Mormonism, I don't think there was much that could compensate for that during my time of transition. That is in no way a criticism of the Christians who were so helpful and supportive to me at that time. I am especially grateful for

115

the prayers that they continually offered for me, and for the prayers for my family that are still being offered.

I think it is important for Christians to stay close to ex-Mormons coming out of the church—to call them frequently and ask how they're doing, and convey willingness to share time with them. At the same time, give them some room to allow the Holy Spirit to work in their lives. Bible studies are helpful, but so is a listening ear for someone who is having problems as a result of their decision to leave Mormonism. My pastor was especially supportive and always willing to help me with questions I had, particularly about Christian doctrine.

I do see several problems with the way Christianity is practiced. The first is a lack of true worship. People seem to be very much "into themselves," and don't seem to really honor the Lord, or live lives that show it. However, I do have good Christian friends who have become involved in my life. They have helped me face problems and live a more spiritual life. I hope to be able to help others in the way that these friends have helped me.

A second problem I see is the division in Christianity over some very important current issues. To me a Christian should not have any questions about creationism, or the sanctity of human life, or about the infallibility of the Scriptures. I believe that being a Christian means accepting the whole Bible as being the Word of God, and that the result will be that you will believe that accepting liberal philosophies and living a worldly life is not God's will for Christians.

Dave Wilkins

I don't miss a thing about Mormonism, but I do think we as Christians should put more emphasis on community outreach. We need to stop saying, "You guys out there are wrong, and we are right," but instead provide an atmosphere where we can say, "Come on in—here's a place where you can have clean entertainment, study, and learn about the family." I really like the trend that many churches have toward putting gyms in their church buildings and getting involved in community activities.

One thing that really eased my transition to Christianity was the fact that the church in Yuma conducted a "New Christians" class that had a really open format. The teacher was never pushy, just helpful. The class was so popular people wanted to repeat it, but you could only take it once! And we had great fellowship outside class, too—dinners together, visiting each other and taking gifts—these involved the whole congregation.

It was that personal touch that really helped LaNell and me. In Mormonism, church leadership shows an interest in individuals and their spiritual well-being, but it is a forced situation because of the interviews. In Christianity it has to be done through developing close friendships.

Cindy Bauer

I guess I miss the zeal that I saw in Mormons.

I also appreciate the honor that they give to their missionaries. In the Mormon church, if you're a missionary, you're a hero. In the Christian church if you're a missionary, most of the time people envision you as a geek who wears funny plaid clothes!

Mormons raise their children with the dream of becoming missionaries. I gave my little brother a bank when he was young that had three compartments: MY TITHE, MY SPENDING MONEY, and MY MISSION. I would hope and pray that every Christian would be open to the challenge of giving between six months and a year to missions, and would raise their children, too, to prepare for a future in missions.

Something else I miss about Mormonism is the way that Mormons recognize the power there is in spoken testimony. Revelation 12:11 speaks of how we are going to defeat the enemy by the blood of the Lamb, and by the word of our testimony, and by not loving our own lives, even unto death. Christians I have seen often lack the boldness in witnessing that comes from practice. Mormons teach their children to "bear their testimonies," and we need to teach our own children to share theirs—not meekly or like they are embarrassed about it, but with courage.

You don't have to have a dramatic conversion experience to tell about—but you can talk about how important Jesus is to you, and what a living, walking relationship means to you.

There are some suggestions I would give to Christians discipling new ex-Mormon believers. The first thing I feel is necessary is to get the new Christian out of the King James Version of the Bible into the New International Version or the New King James Version. The old KJV is, for a Mormon, too locked into mind-patterns that were set when he or she memorized verses connected with Mormon doctrines.

New ex-Mormon Christians need to be encouraged to share their testimonies of the changes God has brought about in their lives. This edifies the Christians who have been praying for them. It should be done without too much fanfare, I think, so as not to push the Mormon into the spotlight too soon or put a burden on him or her that will cause them to have to struggle with the kind of pride that Mormon testimony had fostered in their former life.

Since most Mormons are task-oriented, I also think it is important to give the new Christian a job or a function where they can feel a part of the body. They don't have to become a Bible study leader or such right away, but they should feel useful, too.

Another thing that was very helpful to me was fellowship with other Christians in a small group Bible study once a week. The very best situation possible for an ex-Mormon is to be in such a study with other people who have left Mormonism.

Sheila Garrigus

I still to this day miss my friends, and pray for them. Even now I still miss the closeness found in the Mormon church. Mormons tend to be clannish, but they are also loving and giving and supportive of each other. I am not saying that Christians do not have the same qualities, but I do miss my Mormon friends.

I know from my own experience that when someone leaves the Mormon church, they are so terribly alone. They have a deep need to talk to someone who has been through what they are experiencing.

There is such a spirit of fear associated with leaving Mormonism. Many people face the prospect of losing their mates, their jobs, their friends, their families—that's the meaning of counting the cost. Add to that the fact that you have been taught that the only people who will be in hell are apostates—those who leave the Mormon church.

I know that I probably would not have had the courage to leave the Mormon church, even with all my newfound Christian friends, if I hadn't had John Yount and other ex-Mormons to talk to. I would wake up many nights in desperate fear. And even though John was a Christian radio broadcaster who had to be on the air at 5:30 A.M., he would willingly spend an hour or longer talking with me in the middle of the night. This didn't go on just for days or weeks, but month after month. He was always there when I needed him.

God has been very gracious to me and has allowed me to return that favor by listening to others as they work their way out of Mormonism. I can honestly say that I have never tried to get anybody out of the Mormon church. I do try to lead Mormons to Jesus Christ.

Granny Geer

Of course I miss the fellowship of friends and relatives I left behind in Mormonism, though it is true that Ernest and I have a very good relationship with the Mormons in our own community. Many Mormons (and others) are coming to Jesus through our ministries of publishing, lecturing, and farming. We often share the good news about Jesus along with selling Ernest's luscious watermelons and contaloupes.

But there is one truth that I love to repeat, and that the Christian Body needs to remember: Nobody in the world has the right to hear the story of Jesus twice, before everybody in the world has heard it at least once. I believe a very effective, non-threatening way to reach both Mormons and other non-Christians is through tracts. That way each person can have that opportunity to hear about Jesus.

I remember the lasting effect that the little tract had on me—the one I received by mail about a year before I started going to the Baptist church. Even though I didn't understand all it said, it planted a seed that eventually grew. Now I don't go anywhere—grocery store, airport, anywhere—without tracts to give to people I meet.

It is very important, too, to protect Christians from the deceptive teachings of Mormonism, for I have found that it is much easier to educate a person to keep him from becoming a member of a cult like Mormonism than it is to help that person leave that cult later.

I am happy to come to any community and help lead a tracting team.

Kevin Bond

I felt a real security in Mormonism. Everything was spelled out for me. Everything was either black or white. Now I have a whole painter's palette from which to choose, and it's scary sometimes. But the more I come to understand the fact that God has become my instructor and comforter, and that his law is written in my heart, the more secure I feel.

I have noticed something though about the choices of churches that people make when they leave Mormonism and begin to look for a new place to fellowship. It seems to me that those people who have been most dependent on their former church for control over their lives seem to seek that same thing in a new church. The nature of Mormonism imbedded in people makes them many times drawn to what they left: absolute authority in a church, instant conversion, automatic knowledge.

As to the actual transition though, I think ex-Mormons who are new Christians would have an easier time of it if people would recognize that it is hard to make changes in basic beliefs. I had a friend who left Mormonism and was visiting different churches. Once in conversation with a group of Christians, he casually mentioned something about Satan and Jesus being brothers. Talk about a show-stopper! But they were patient with him and told him the truth (which of course he couldn't just absorb by osmosis—he had to be taught).

Once after I visited a certain church the minister came to our home. I asked some questions—honest questions—about their views on the Trinity. The pastor became very angry. He thought I was challenging his presentation of basic doctrine, when I was just asking some earnest questions. I was a brand-new Christian and that just devastated me.

Sandra Tanner

When I left Mormonism, I was terribly lonely. Everyone I had associated with was Mormon, and so I left behind all my friends, my family, my social life. No one was violent or anything like that—it was more a matter of shunning, of becoming invisible in the community.

The same is true today. When an active Mormon leaves, he leaves something that involved a great amount of his time. Then suddenly he has great chunks of uncommitted time. There must be individuals in the Christian community who are willing to take up the slack in this very difficult time.

Many times Mormons who discover the false nature of their religion become disillusioned and conclude, "If Mormonism isn't true, nothing is," and turn their backs on everything. This is the critical time for them, when they need personal contact with Christians.

I believe that here in the Salt Lake Valley there are many hurting, dissatisfied Mormons who believe that there could be something better, but who don't know where to look. They are too intimidated to walk out on their own, or to walk into a Christian church alone. The Christian community has to be willing to really stretch, to bridge the gap between the Mormon ward house and the Christian church building, to prepare them through friendship and conversation for what will be an initially strange experience the first time they worship with Christians.

I've seen through the years that the people who come out of Mormonism and go on to be faithful Christians have, almost without exception, a close Christian friend. Very few people who study their way out of Mormonism on their own actually go on to find Christianity unless there's been someone in their lives to live it out before them.

As a Mormon is in contact with such a Christian who relies on God and turns to him for strength, what should happen is that the Mormon will have an increasing longing to have that same relationship and to follow God as he is revealed in the Bible. But it takes time to work through what this really means. Many times Christians become really impatient for a Mormon to move faster, but each person has to mature at his own rate.

For instance, a person may accept Christ and still hang on to some remnants of Mormonism. In this case, the Christian who is working with him should emphasize that everything must square with the Bible: if someone will agree to that, then the Holy Spirit will work the rest of Mormonism out of him, as long as he is willing to make the Bible the sole criterion for what he believes.

I don't recommend that ex-Mormons attend the bishop's court when they decide to leave the church. Most new Christians don't need the kind of pressure that is put on them there. I think you can do a better job of telling why you left Mormonism in a letter, which will be read and remembered. Neither Jerald nor I had particularly good experiences when we attended the bishops' courts at our own excommunications, and feel we could have made a greater impact for Christ with a letter.

Latayne Scott

Partly as the result of persecution, and partly because of their own peculiar doctrines and practices, Mormons have a sense of community, an us-against-the-world mentality that binds them together even more strongly than race or nationality can.

As I look at Christianity as it is practiced today, I think some churches have lost the identity that distinguishes them from the world. They are accepted by the world because they are like the world—and that is horribly incriminating. I fear that it might take a time of persecution of the church for us to be able to pull together as we should.

Since that sense of community does not exist in some Christian churches, I believe that individuals within those bodies can provide a place of nurturing of new Christians (especially those who are ex-Mormons) by forming small "care groups" who meet together regularly in homes to study the Bible, pray for each other, and meet each other's needs. I don't mean this should necessarily replace membership in a larger fellowship, but should supplement and enhance it.

13

Current Worship Experiences

Where do you now worship?

How do you feel about people of other Christian denominations?

Randy Steele

I attend a Christian and Missionary Alliance church. I don't believe that only one denomination is right. There are others, I know, who worship the Lord as Savior. But those people who doubt the inerrancy of the Bible or who advocate things that the Bible opposes, I believe are lost or at least greatly misled in their Christian faith.

Dave Wilkins

I worship at the Montgomery Boulevard Church of Christ in Albuquerque, New Mexico. I try to be as accepting as I can of people of other denominations because God will accept or reject them, and I would hate to reject someone God has accepted. When people don't believe the same way I do, I like to study with them, find out where we can agree, and where we don't. Then look at the Bible and see what we can do about it.

Cindy Bauer

I presently worship at an Assembly of God. The church that I consider my home church in Hawaii, where I have lived most of my Christian life, is Grace Bible Church in Honolulu, an independent church that most people would say is somewhat pentecostal in nature.

I choose to remain interdenominational, because of my ministry to Mormons. But I can feel a part of any God-fearing, Bible-preaching, Jesus-loving, cross-clinging church that believes in 1 Corinthians 15:3. I have ministered in churches of just about every denomination I can think of.

Sheila Garrigus

I worship at Eastside Baptist Church in Marietta, Georgia.

When asked, I say that I'm a Christian. Jim and I have spoken and taught in churches of almost every denomination. I have no problem with denominations. I see what we as believers all have in common and that is so much more important than our differences. What it comes down to is that we are all sinners saved by the blood of Jesus Christ, and that is what matters.

Nothing else is really important. To me, it is immaterial if one church sprinkles and other chooses immersion; if one speaks in tongues and another doesn't—as long as we focus on the cross and Jesus, we are one.

Granny Geer

Ernest and I still worship at the same Baptist church where I was born again almost a half-century ago.

I witness in churches all over the United States, as well as in other nations. I regard as my brothers and sisters those people who trust only in the saving blood of Jesus Christ for their salvation as I do. I learn a great deal from people of other fellowships—especially that God is no respecter of persons, and that he loves people of all races.

Kevin Bond

My family and I worship at Southeast Baptist Church. We believe that they are conservative and Bible-based—a combination we need.

I think denominational differences are in one way good. There is unity in the diversity of the church, just as there is in the Trinity.

However, when these differences are cherished as defensive boundaries to be guarded—ways to keep others out—then they are bad. I believe people are led by the Spirit to those bodies or congregations where they will be most effective and most happy. From that point on, they should conscientiously try to build bridges to people of other Christian denominations.

Sandra Tanner

Jerald and I and our family have been members of the Christian and Missionary Alliance Church, where we have attended for almost twenty-five years.

When a Mormon comes to me who is searching for truth, I tell them to look for a church that is faithful to the Bible. Now I believe that it is very important that Christian churches be unified in their efforts to reach Mormons, without dividing over denominational lines. But I try to prepare Mormons for the fact that not all churches are faithful to the Bible: some do not believe the whole Bible, don't believe Jesus was really resurrected, modify the gospel. I also emphasize that salvation is an individual matter, not just an issue of where one goes to church.

Latayne Scott

I worship at the Mountainside Church of Christ in Albuquerque, New Mexico. I have worshiped with the same body of people all the years I have lived here.

As far as fellowship is concerned, I do not want to bind anything on believers that the New Testament does not require. I believe that anyone who seriously studies the examples of conversions in the Book of Acts will conclude that baptism is part of the believer's conversion, and is inextricably bound together with commitment to Jesus Christ. For that reason, I encourage anyone I know who makes a decision for Christ to identify himself or herself with his death, burial, and resurrection as pictured in baptism (Rom. 6:3–5). We are all travelers on the road to salvation, and we all can learn. I especially am always learning; and I try to extend the same loving acceptance toward others that I would like to receive.

14

Advice for Concerned Christians

Based on your own experience, what advice would you give to a Christian who is trying to influence a Mormon for Christ?

Are there any teaching techniques that you feel are particularly effective in leading Mormons to Christ?

Which is more important, do you think, in teaching a Mormon; using the Bible or showing inconsistencies in Mormon doctrine?

Randy Steele

The first important step the Christian should take is to pray for the Mormon, and enlist the prayers of others to pray for him or her.

Then I think the believer should really internalize the teachings of Ephesians 6:11–17, which talks about the nature of the battle, and how to arm oneself for it.

In the actual teaching situation the Christian must remember to present the truth with sincerity, and without contentiousness—that is, without arguments or shouting because these things will never win anyone to Christ.

Any Christian who shares with a member of a cult must know his or her own faith, and be prepared to explain and defend it, always using Scripture to prove each point.

At each point where a Mormon might think he has answers out of the Bible, show him the verse in context, show him parallel passages, and use supporting passages.

Mormons need to also be confronted with the truth about Mormonism: the changes in their own scripture, the deceit that characterized the early days of that church, and the cover-ups that the church is using even today. These can be shared in a loving, noncondemning way.

Dave Wilkins

First of all don't be pushy and don't come on with a holier-than-thou attitude. As Larry did with us, just teach the Bible. Don't dig at the other person's personal beliefs. It's all right to point out differences but always remember to give the other person a chance to respond. Say, "What do you think about that?" or "What is the reason or logic here?"

Above all, become friends and as much as possible, let the other person know how much you care about him or her personally. The best teaching technique is based on getting to know the other person and not coming on too strong.

As far as an actual teaching method is concerned, the course of study Larry used with me was called "Open Bible Study"—a series of pamphlets. I realize that teaching just the Bible may not be too effective with Mormons who don't believe it's translated correctly. On the other hand showing them inconsistencies in Mormon doctrine sometimes doesn't work either—for instance, my family responds by saying, "Well, if the prophet says it, that's the way it is, consistent or not."

Cindy Bauer

The most important, powerful thing you can do is to share your own testimony of what Jesus Christ has done in your life. Make sure this includes your conversion experience, telling of your past and how God changed you. Share experiences of how he helped you with finances, or healing, or just in your daily walk.

Always come to a Mormon with a humble, loving spirit, with the vanguard of the prayers of others to support you. Read all you can about Mormonism. Don't "ambush" a Mormon. Tell them up front that you are witnessing to them, and why. Don't use ridicule or derision. Ask questions; help the Mormon to see things for himself for herself: "Have you seen this?" "What do you think of this?" "How does this fit with what you have been taught?"

Never witness to a Mormon alone, and never, never attend their meetings with them. Do not go to their activities with them, but be in control of who meets where. Take them to spirit-filled worship services and meetings where they can feel and see the excitement of Christians who love their God and enjoy worshiping him.

Show your Mormon friend how Christians pray for each other. Don't be afraid to talk about your own prayer life. I can remember when I was a Mormon, hearing an official proclamation from Salt Lake City that said that the opening prayer for a "prayer meeting" that would precede a Sunday School or other auxiliary meetings should be no longer than something like ninety seconds, and that the benediction shouldn't be any longer than forty-five seconds. I may not have a completely accurate memory of those time limitations, but I remember acutely the message: Get it over with. So the idea of sustained prayer is often novel to a Mormon who needs to see it in action.

When I was attending the Melodyland church, there was a class that was aimed at exposing the errors of cults. I learned a lot in that class, and wish more churches would teach such a class.

If at all possible, get your Mormon friend in direct contact with an ex-Mormon Christian. The Christian who sets up the meeting should open his or her home and make the Mormon as comfortable as possible.

Challenge the Mormon to read both the Bible and literature about Mormonism with an open mind. Many people have also been helped by seeing the videos, *The Godmakers* and *Temple of the Godmakers*.

Remember that the Mormon has no understanding of sin as we know it; he understands the concept of right and wrong, but sin has little meaning for him. Mormon doctrine also equates what we call salvation with the combination of faith and works, so they are never completely sure they've done "enough" to earn it.

I think it is important to point out contradictions between the Bible and Mormon doctrine, as well as the contradictions with the Mormon scriptures themselves—like the scripture in the *Book of Mormon* (Moroni 8:18), which states that God is "unchangeable from all eternity to all eternity" (which conflicts with standard LDS doctrine that he was once a man).

Of course, there is a danger—you can get someone disenchanted, convinced that Mormonism is wrong, and yet not lead them to Christ. Seeing Mormonism is wrong has to be accompanied by constant, loving exposure to Jesus Christ.

The biggest witnessing tool a Christian has is his own life of a victorious walk with Christ—one that shows sanctification and the righteousness of God. The Mormons I have known have been good parents, good housekeepers, Mothers of the Year, faithful in church attendance, and clean living. They're not going to be motivated to leave all that if you try to talk to them with a cup of coffee in one hand and a cigarette in the other. Christians who live their lives during the week like they do on Sunday—reading their Bibles, praying earnestly, living a moral life—are the ones a Mormon will listen to.

Sheila Garrigus

When I witness to Mormons, I use the Bible, God's Word. And when need be, I use LDS books. I use my own personal testimony.

When I was a Mormon, I thought Christians were hypocrites. I saw them saying one thing and doing another. A Mormon must see Jesus in the person who is witnessing to him or her.

I try to be as honest as I can when I am talking to a Mormon. I never compare Mormonism to any other church. In fact, I don't talk about church at all; I talk about a Person. I am there to introduce the Mormon to my friend, Jesus; my Savior, Jesus. I am not there to introduce them to another organization.

As far as doctrine goes, I tend to stick to discussing the personhood of God the Father, and Jesus Christ the Son. Most Mormons do not realize how greatly Christianity differs on their personhoods and on the plan of salvation. Once they see that there are indeed two different gospels involved, then I start sharing with them about Jesus.

I ask them, "What do you believe about Jesus? Who is he to you? What do his life and death mean to you?" I ask questions. And then I share my testimony of what he has done in my life, and the changes he has made there.

I share verses with them from the Bible, and I always ask them to read. I point out the context of the verse in question as it relates to the entire chapter where it appears.

I learned this from the people in two small group Bible studies I attended. Never once did they attack the Mormon church. Never once did they ridicule what I believed. But they were very firm whenever I made a statement that was not biblically correct. They would take me to the Bible and read the verses in context, or make me do it. They had Bible study aids, with Greek and Hebrew, and let me see things for myself. They didn't tell me—they showed me, leading me gently but firmly.

Jesus, when he came into my life, did it gently and slowly and lovingly. He did not pounce on me, and I don't pounce on Mormons.

Granny Geer

I find the most expedient and least antagonistic way to witness to a Mormon is to share certain Mormon doctrines with them that will shake their faith in Mormonism. I call such things "grabbers" and "shockers."

One way I do this is to show them how they have been taught to sing lies in church. After I discuss with a Mormon the virgin birth, for instance, I will ask them why they sing "Round yon virgin, Mother and child," when so many of them have told me that although Mary was a virgin when God came to her, she was not a virgin when he left her—so, she couldn't be a virgin and be a mother at the same time. Official LDS doctrine denies the virgin birth.

My book *Mormonism, Mama, and Me!* is full of "grabbers." Many of them have to do with the Mormon view of God. Sometimes I just try to get Mormons to stop and think about some of the implication of their beliefs. For instance, since they believe that God eats and drinks like a man, then I ask them if he also digests food (*see* Orson Pratt, *The Seer*, vol. 1, no. 3*)*. When they admit that he must, then I ask them if there are "comfort stations" in heaven. Usually their response is, "I never thought of that!" My book also discusses false ideas found in Mormon sermons such as Adam was sexually conceived and born; Adam is the husband of Mary and the procreative father of Jesus; Mormon gods and goddesses are eating and digesting celestial vegetables, which allows them to have spirit babies (*see* Orson Pratt, *The Seer*, vol. 1, no. 3).

I am preparing a book titled, *Mormonism's Salvation: By Grace or by Sex?* which is a greatly expanded version of a tract I wrote by the same name. It includes quotations from prominent Mormons such as Brigham Young and Bruce R. McConkie. It shows that Mormonism teaches that not only God, Jesus Christ, the Holy Ghost and Satan were sexually begotten, but so were angels and demons. It also exposes the false theory that the virgin Mary, when resurrected, could be one of God's wives to bear him spirit children in eternity!

The typical Mormon response when hearing such things is, "Well, the church doesn't teach that anymore—that's from the 1800s." Then I have an opportunity to ask them who they believe—Brigham Young or one of their current prophets who has changed their "everlasting gospel." In fact, I offer a twelve-thousand-dollar reward to the first Latter-day Saint who can prove that the Mormon doctrines I discuss in my books and tracts were never taught by Mormon authorities.

Too many Mormons don't know or understand what Mormonism really is, so it sometimes takes several sessions to show them the truth, and get them to fully trust the Bible. After all the *Book of Mormon* in 2 Nephi 29:6 teaches that anyone who trusts in the Bible is a "fool." But I use the Bible anyway, as much as I can—as much as they will let me—and tell them how precious it is to me.

Kevin Bond

The first point to remember is to do it prayerfully. Resolve to be both gentle and honest. Then when you sit down with the Mormon, do it as a fellow student not as a teacher. "Here's how I understand this passage" you might say, "but let's both sit down as students and look at it together. I'm curious to know how you feel about it." Then listen carefully to what they have to say—not just to their vocabulary but to their hearts. When Scripture is the teacher in that kind of situation and the Holy Spirit is the tutor, you both can learn.

I remember the gentle and persistently loving way that Jane Tallant shared Scripture with me. Years later I would hear something and the memory of what she had said would click together with it, even though I hadn't understood what she was saying at the time.

Something else to remember is that Mormons do not understand a lot of our "church words." When we talk to them about "getting saved" or "walking the aisle" or "accepting the Lord into your heart," these terms that are supercharged for us are practically meaningless to them. If I find myself using "church words" with a Mormon, I try to stop and tell them what those phrases mean to me.

I also try to always carry with me a King James Bible to share Scripture with Mormons. It's small and lightweight and not threatening. I not only have key scriptures marked but I have written in the margins plenty of references and cross-references to make it an effective "sword," because the first thing a Mormon will say when you confront him or her with truth is "Where does it say that?"

My advice would be to treat Mormons like you treat a baby who is going from the bottle to solid food. When you pull the bottle of Mormon doctrine out of their mouths, you have to be ready right then with the spoon of truth to feed them. So I definitely advocate a combination of Scripture with showing the errors in Mormon doctrine.

Sandra Tanner

Ultimately, the fact that Jerald was sincere in his commitment to Christ was a big factor in making me want to listen to him. He wasn't just bashing Mormonism, but he truly had a faith in God outside of Mormonism. As I visited different churches, I could see people there who also truly had a relationship with Christ that was different from just being a member there. I saw the depth of their sincerity, their commitment, their prayers. Seeing that warmness of their fellowship with God drew my spirit to look for something more.

I think that using the Bible and showing the inconsistencies in Mormonism go hand in hand. I had to see the inconsistencies in Mormon doctrine in order to be able to take the Bible seriously. As long as I perceived Mormonism as a consistent whole, without problems, I saw no reason to look outside it for answers. At some point I had to be challenged on the reliability of Mormonism and Joseph Smith before I could have a reason for caring to learn about someone else's faith.

An increasing percentage of the Mormons with whom I come into contact are disillusioned and already have doubts, so I don't have to spend the time I used to showing that Mormonism is wrong. But if they are still locked into Mormon thought, it becomes obvious when I ask them to define some of the terms they use. From that point we can have a productive discussion about what our source of authority is, how truth is determined, who do we look to for answers, how authoritative is the Bible, and what else could be more authoritative than the Bible.

A Mormon will eventually fall back on Joseph Smith and his claim to new revelation. At that point I challenge, "How can we trust the word of Joseph Smith when he continually changed it and contradicted himself? Where can I be sure to get truth?" The Mormon, who believes that the Bible is unreliable because it has been changed, looks to church leaders. I then show proof of how all Mormon scriptures have been changed, which undermines the authority of the church leaders who advocate them.

Latayne Scott

My advice on teaching a Mormon depends entirely on how much time I anticipate spending with that Mormon. If it is only one "shot" (say, witnessing to someone like a missionary that you believe you will never see again), I believe the most important thing you can tell that Mormon is that you are happy as a Christian, that you are satisfied and fulfilled.

Why is that important? As a Mormon I believed that all Christians felt a great void in their lives that could only be filled by Mormonism. I couldn't imagine being satisfied with just one book of Scripture, or without continuing revelation from an up-to-date prophet, or without eternal marriage—and so I transferred those feelings to Christians I met. It would have been very jarring to me to hear from the lips of a Christian that he or she was truly secure in the Lord.

Just think of the cumulative effect that such a testimony would have on a couple of Mormon missionaries who are tracting down a street in your neighborhood, if each Christian who answered the door had a radiant smile and could tell them how blessed they were to belong to the Lord!

I believe that 2 John clearly teaches that we should not welcome anyone into our home who doesn't bring Christ's teaching. But a fervent witness of the goodness of our God and our love for him can have more effect than ten "studies" with two young missionaries who are specifically commanded to teach and not be taught *(Doctrine and Covenants* 43:15).

The situation is different with someone with whom I can have an ongoing study, who is willing to listen. Such a person still needs to know that I am happy and fulfilled as a Christian, and needs to see my Christianity in action in my home and in my life. But in addition to that, I have often used a certain technique, recommended by longtime missionary to Mormons, John L. Smith, that is very disarming and nonthreatening to a Mormon. I will ask a Mormon how important the *Book of Mormon* is in his or her life. The answer is always that the *Book of Mormon* restored the lost gospel to the earth and was so important, in fact, that Joseph Smith and others were willing to die for it.

Then I ask the Mormon to describe what God is like. He or she will enjoy telling about the deity with body, parts, and passions who lives near the star Kolob, who was once a man on an earth like ours. I try to draw out as many details as possible, writing them down if I can.

Then I ask them to find those things about God in the *Book of Mormon*. (They are not there because Joseph Smith wrote the *Book of Mormon* before he formulated his theories on God that are so unbiblical.)

Thus, without any criticism or introduction of "anti-Mormon literature," you can make your point about an inconsistency in Mormon doctrine. Later, as the person is willing to listen, you can share passages from the Bible (Isaiah chapters 43 and 44 are especially good here) and show other inconsistencies in doctrine.

15

Helpful Books
for Decision Making

What books, literature, speakers, were most helpful and effective to you personally during your time of decision and transition from Mormonism?

Which would you recommend for Christians?

Which for Mormons?

Randy Steele

The books that interested me most when I was coming out of Mormonism were those which revealed the true nature of the church, as evidenced by doctrines such as blood atonement, plurality of wives, and other doctrines that the church today tries to deny in its history. Such books really upset me, but were probably what helped change my mind most quickly.

The Tanners' *Mormonism: Shadow or Reality?*, Bob Witte's book *Where Does It Say That?* (Ex-Mormons for Jesus, Brockton, Massachusetts) and Latayne Scott's book *The*

Mormon Mirage were particularly helpful early on for me. Also, the video *The Mormon Dilemma* is a good one to share with Mormons. There was a time where I read nothing but books on Mormonism—from the ones I mentioned, to Walter Martin, to Granny Geer—everything I could get my hands on. After I settled in my own mind the true nature of Mormonism, then I started to read about Christianity. The book that helped me most was Josh McDowell's *Evidence That Demands a Verdict* (Campus Crusade, 1979). I also have enjoyed reading different Bible commentaries because of the insight they give me into difficult Bible passages.

I would recommend that anyone who is teaching a Mormon be familiar with the books I have mentioned that are testimonies of people coming out of Mormonism, and also be familiar with *Mormonism: Shadow or Reality?* and Jim Spencer's book, *Have You Witnessed to a Mormon Lately?* (Chosen Books, 1987).

Books given to Mormons should be gentle, raising questions about Mormon history and doctrine in a way that is not harsh. I think books that show the inerrancy of the Bible would be good, too.

Dave Wilkins

The Bible was it for me. Talk about power in the Word—there is! I wouldn't read anything but the Bible for several years after I became a Christian. I broke that rule for myself once, I think, and I regretted it.

As for recommended reading for Mormons, I don't recommend anything in particular. The anti-Mormon books I ran into when I was still a Mormon didn't shake my faith; they just made me a little angry because I felt like the church was being picked on. My older brother really gets upset about that kind of book—considers it a personal affront.

Cindy Bauer

I encourage Mormons to read the Psalms. They helped me see God and to worship him as the mighty, all-powerful deity who was, and is, and is to come. And, of course, the Gospels are essential. The Book of Galatians helped me a lot, too.

Personal testimony books that I read were excellent. I recommend *Youth Aflame* by Winkey Pratney (Bethany, 1983); *Hind's Feet on High Places* by Hannah Hurnard (Tyndale, 1979); and books by Corrie ten Boom such as *The Hiding Place* (Revell, 1971), *Tramp for the Lord* (Revell, 1974) and *In My Father's House* (Revell, 1976). My number-one recommendation is *Prison to Praise* by Merlin R. Carothers (Carothers, 1970).

Of course, I will always be indebted to the anonymous man who handed me that tract on Temple Square. I know that one day in heaven my Savior Lord Jesus will introduce me to that man, and I will rejoice with him around the throne of God, thanking God for that man, and for that tract, that little "paper missionary."

As far as speakers who influenced me during that time, Dr. Walter Martin would very definitely top the list. Also very influential were Marian and Jerry Bodine, my class teachers at Melodyland. I enjoyed the concerts my Christian friends invited me to, and think that in many ways Christian music was the best "literature" for me.

Sheila Garrigus

Some of the books Jim bought that were helpful to me were *The Cross and the Switchblade* by David Wilkerson (Spire, 1987); *High Adventure* by George Otis (Revell, 1971); and *A New Song* by Pat Boone (Creation House, 1970). The personal testimonies of these people were very influential on me.

I've given *The Mormon Mirage* to a lot of Mormons. I also really like Floyd McElveen's *Will the "Saints" Go Marching In?* (Regal Books, 1977) and Fawn Brodie's *No Man Knows My History* (Knopf, 1971). And, of course, anything by Jerald and Sandra Tanner is factual and well researched.

I think Walter Martin's books are outstanding, but a lot of Mormons won't read anything of his—it's just like a red flag to them. Usually I just stick to the Bible and their own books of scripture.

I also know many ex-Mormons who love music, and it has been very effective in ministering to them. Books, music—they're tools, and we have to realize that God's best tools are yielded Christians who let the Lord use them.

Granny Geer

Well, of course, forty years ago there weren't many materials that dealt directly with Mormonism. But that one tract, "You Must Be Born Again," was very influential, and when I was privileged to meet its author, Pastor P. D. O'Brien, about six months after I came to the Lord, I hugged his neck and thanked him for what he had done for me!

Then, when I had been a Christian about three weeks, my in-laws gave me the little booklet called *Mormonism Under the Searchlight*. It really helped me see how ungodly are the secret tenets of Mormonism that I had loved so long. However, it was written with a such a harsh, sarcastic tone that it shouldn't be given to Mormons.

But of course, the Bible was the dearest, most influential book then, and still is to me.

Kevin Bond

I cannot recommend highly enough Josh McDowell's *Evidence That Demands a Verdict*. I have given many copies of it away because it is so factual and rational. I also really benefited from F. F. Bruce's *The New Testament Documents: Are They Reliable?* (InterVarsity, 1973); McDowell's other book, *More Than A Carpenter* (Tyndale, 1980); and Miles J. Stanford's *The Green Letters* (Zondervan, 1975), a series that helps one develop a status with Christ, and then to maintain it; and C. S. Lewis's *Mere Christianity* (Macmillan, 1952).

As for books dealing with Mormonism: *The Mormon Mirage* is always powerful because it has a nice, soft touch. I recommend the Tanners' *Mormonism: Shadow or Reality?* and Walter Martin's *Kingdom of the Cults* (Bethany, 1985). Marvin Cowan's *Mormon Claims Answered* (Cowan, 1982) is a little book that has been very helpful to me.

The speaker that had the greatest influence on me is Billy Graham.

Sandra Tanner

You have to realize that when I came out of Mormonism, there was very little available! I remember reading David Whitmer's pamphlet, "An Address to All Believers in Christ," which though it was written over a hundred years ago had a great impact on me. This, combined with the photocopies that Jerald had of original Mormon documents that clearly showed inconsistencies in both Mormon history as well as doctrine, was all the "anti-Mormon" literature I saw.

Today of course the situation is very different. There are several excellent books that I would give to a Mormon. Floyd McElveen's *Mormon Illusion* (Regal, 1985) is a good book, as is *The Mormon Mirage*. Jerald and I have written *The Changing World of Mormonism* and *Major Problems of Mormonism* in such a way that they could be given to a Mormon. Four other books that I would recommend and could give to a Mormon friend are Ed Gruss's *What Every Mormon Should Know* (Accent Books, 1976), Marvin Cowan's *Mormon Claims Answered*, Jim Spencer's *Beyond Mormonism: An Elder's Story* (Revell, 1984), and Harry Ropp's *Are the Mormon Scriptures Reliable?* (InterVarsity, 1987).

There are other books and tapes available, too, that have good information in them. Some of them though are harsh and critical in tone and don't show a respect or compassion for Mormon people. Christians can read these for the information, but the negative tone should keep you from giving them to your Mormon friend.

Latayne Scott

The first literature I ever saw exposing Mormonism was a green and white tract by someone named Larry Jonas. I don't remember the title, but I can still see it in my mind, in spite of the fact that I threw it away because its teachings that Mormonism was not of God upset me so much. It wasn't until eight or nine years later that I left Mormonism, and I think that little tract paved the way and helped me be open to the books I read later.

The books that most heavily influenced me when I was making a decision were *What Does The Book of Mormon Teach?* by Gordon Fraser (Moody, 1964); *The Book of Mormon?* by James D. Bales (Old Paths Book Club, 1958); *No Man Knows My History* by Fawn Brodie; and *Mormonism: Shadow or Reality?* by Jerald and Sandra Tanner. I believe the first two are out of print, but I highly recommend all of them to both Christians and Mormons.

16

Helpful Resources
for Nurturing

**Since you have become a Christian, which books, litera-
ture, speakers, have been most helpful or edifying to
you?**

Randy Steele

A Bible with a good commentary or notes in it is important to me. My first Bible was a *Ryrie Study Bible* in the
New King James Version that was very helpful to me, but
now I use a *NIV Study Bible*.

I also picked up a book I like called *God's Word Made
Plain* by Mrs. Paul Friederichsen (Moody, 1958). Its subtitle
is "Bird's Eye View Bible Course."

A part of the Bible that has been very significant to me is
the book of Leviticus. Learning the truth about the priesthood and even the Christological meaning of the real temple's functions and furnishings really convicted me of the
truth of the Bible.

I have enjoyed the John Ankerberg television show with
its programs on different cults, and I love the Zola Levitt
show and the teachings of Charles Stanley. On the radio, I

listen to John McArthur, Chuck Swindoll, James Dobson, and really enjoyed the late J. Vernon McGee.

Dave Wilkins

The William Barclay series of New Testament commentaries, *The Daily Study Bible,* have been very helpful to me, even though I see problems with some of his views. I use them extensively for background information when I am preparing to teach classes.

James Dobson has had real effect on me as far as building Christian unity and family relationships. Dr. Carl Breechen and Dr. Paul Faulkner of Abilene Christian University also have been helpful.

But I always go back to the Bible—that's where I put my emphasis. If you go back to it and think about it, give yourself plenty of time to think about it and all the ramifications of a lesson you might teach from it, that's where the edifying comes from. I think about it, read it, and try to apply it.

Cindy Bauer

I would recommend for Christians any of the excellent books that Jim Spencer has written on Mormonism. My husband also distributes a lot of copies of Thelma Geer's *Mormonism, Mama, and Me!* The books that Jerald and Sandra Tanner have written are especially informative for Christians who want to know more about Mormonism.

We are opening up a base in Utah and are recommending that our workers read the novels of Marian Wells, an author who grew up in Utah as a Nazarene. These books are very insightful.

I Dared to Call Him Father by Bilquis Sheikh, a former Muslim (Chosen Books, 1980); *Death of a Guru* by Rabindranath R. Maharaj and Dave Hunt (Harvest House, 1986); *Sit, Walk, Stand* by Watchman Nee (Tyndale, 1988); and *This Present Darkness* by Frank Peretti (Crossway, 1986) are books that I have recently read and recommend.

I have also benefited greatly from Ed Decker's work, and that of Dave Hunt and Ron Carlson.

Granny Geer

I think the book, *Concerned Christians Witness to Mormons* (Concerned Christians, Inc., Mesa, AZ, 1983), is a very, very good book. It clearly shows that while Mormon scripture may agree with the Bible, Mormon doctrine does not.

Other books I recommend are *The Mormon Mirage* by Latayne Scott, *Mormon Claims Answered* by Marvin Cowan, *Understanding Mormonism* (Truth in Love Ministries of Lake Oswego, Oregon), *Where Does It Say That?* by Bob Witte, John L. Smith's *Witnessing Effectively to Mormons* (Utah Missions, 1975), and the books written by the Tanners.

A new book, really excellent, by Linda LeHanson called *Christian Defense Against Mormon Attacks* (In His Time Ministry, 1987) is one that I'm finding the most helpful in exposing such doctrines as Mormonism's proposed emasculation (in the resurrection) of all non-temple-married men. I also use in my ministry a pamphlet called *What's Going On in There?* by Chuck Sackett.

Of course, I use my own book most extensively and effectively. Anyone who would like to obtain copies of *Mormonism, Mama, and Me!*, *A Christian Defense Against Mormon Attacks*, or any of the video or audio tapes that contain my testimony, or tracts, can write me directly at Rt. 2 Box 723, Safford, AZ 85546, or phone me at (602) 428-2380.

Other most helpful and powerful tools in witnessing to Mormons are the Jeremiah films (16 mm and video) *The Godmakers*, *Temple of the Godmakers*, and *Godmakers II* (soon to be released). They are available from Jeremiah Films, PO Box 1712, Hemet, CA 92343; (800) 828-2290.

Kevin Bond

First and foremost, Scripture has been the most influential because of its great power. I also enjoy devotional books like those by Oswald Chambers and books on church history. J. I. Packer's *Knowing God* (InterVarsity, 1973) has had a great impact on my life.

The speakers I enjoy most now are Josh McDowell, Billy Graham, and Charles Stanley.

I do read about Mormonism, but I think that can be over-done. I have friends who have left the Mormon church whose main topic of conversation even years afterward is, "Can you believe that Joseph Smith said such and such." While that is valid and interesting, it should not be the focus of your life! A Christian can talk about all the good things God is doing now without wallowing in the past and its pain.

Sandra Tanner

I believe that a new Christian should read books that accomplish two things: build his confidence and faith in the Bible, and give him some sort of systematic overview of doctrine in the Bible. I recommend *Know What You Believe* (Victor, 1985) and *Know Why You Believe* (Victor, 1984) by Paul Little and *Basic Christianity* by John R. W. Stott. A good devotional book for either Mormons or Christians is *Knowing God* by Packer. Those who are good readers will also benefit from F. F. Bruce's *The New Testament Documents: Are They Reliable?* (Eerdmans, 1983).

Latayne Scott

I try to listen regularly to J. Vernon McGee, Charles Stanley, and John McArthur. I also really appreciate Landon Saunders.

Books about Mormonism that have helped me include Floyd McElveen's *Will the "Saints" Go Marching In?*, *Where Does It Say That?* by Bob Witte, *The Book of Mormon: True or False?* by Arthur Budvarson (Pacific Publishing Co., 1974), and anything that Jerald and Sandra Tanner publish—books, newsletters—anything.

My favorite authors now are C. S. Lewis (especially *Mere Christianity* and *A Grief Observed* [Seabury, 1963]), Tim Stafford (*Knowing the Face of God* [Zondervan, 1986]), and Phillip Yancey (*Where Is God When It Hurts* [Zondervan, 1977], *Fearfully and Wonderfully Made* [Zondervan, 1987], *Disappointment With God* [Zondervan, 1988]).

My Bible (NIV version), though, is my best reading companion.

17

Effective Nurturing Techniques

Is there anything that you would say to the Christian body as a whole about Mormonism, teaching Mormons, and nurturing ex-Mormons who are new Christians?

Randy Steele

Many Christians believe that Mormonism is nothing dangerous—that it should be accepted by all as another Christian denomination. That one particular error in thinking will allow Mormonism to gain a greater foothold into the Christian community than any other one assumption.

The Mormon church feeds on people who are searching. If the church they are attending doesn't believe in the Bible as God's inerrant word, or has liberal influences that foster their doubts, then they will be drawn to a church that says it has all the answers. Mormonism thrives on insecurity.

A Christian who is strong in his faith and in the Bible may not be threatened by Mormonism. But, Christian, what about your family, your friends, your neighbors who are not as strong as you? Mormonism will teach them that "Christendom was hatched in hell," and that there is no

148

salvation outside the Mormon church. Its goal is not to make everyone Christians—it is to make everyone Mormons; not to convert people to the true Christ, but to give them a testimony of Joseph Smith.

To any reader who is coming out of Mormonism, all I can say is, God bless you. You have chosen right. God will honor you for your decision, though you may be in for some rough times. As one who has been where you are, I have empathy for you. I know what you are going through, and it is not easy. Some of you face trials in your life, opposition from friends or relatives, or maybe even a spouse who does not accept your decision. But here is what I would share with you, to close my story and my testimony:

> And God shall wipe away all tears from their eyes; and there shall be no more death, neither sorrow nor crying; neither shall there be any more pain: for the former things are passed away (Rev. 21:4, KJV).

Dave Wilkins

My advice about Mormonism is *watch out for it*. We need to be more aware of not only what Mormons teach but of how they use words. They use words we know, like *salvation*, but it doesn't have the same meaning when they say that word. Also, when Mormon missionaries go in to teach a family, they don't tell them the whole truth. They only teach the part that somebody with a Christian background can accept. They don't tell you right off that you can "become a god" or about the changes in their doctrine and history.

There are groups like Ex-Mormons For Jesus who can really help educate the Christian community to these things. We need to utilize these ministries.

Once a Mormon leaves the church and becomes a Christian, he or she needs to be nurtured slowly. Accept that Mormons are going to have some way-out ideas. (I still do!) As to activity level for the new ex-Mormon Christian—get them as involved as they want to be without feeling like they are back into the hierarchy they just escaped. Let them enjoy their newfound freedom in Christ.

Cindy Bauer

I remember after I got saved, I asked God, "Why did you save me? Why didn't you save Donnie and Marie, or the president of the Mormon church, or someone really famous within Mormonism that would really shake the foundations of many people?"

I believe the Lord answered that question very powerfully to me by telling me that my salvation was due to the intercessory prayers of Christians who had beaten back the demonic forces that held me captive with deceptions like seeing my chest on fire and believing the lies of Mormon doctrine.

If I could convey one message to Christians, it is that it is absolutely vital to maintain personal time daily with the Lord, worshiping and praising and praying.

The other essential is spending time daily in God's Word. It is food to our souls, and without it we will fail. Statistics show that less than 10 percent of Christians read their Bibles daily.

We must be involved in local churches, reaching out, and loving one another. We must learn to forgive.

Finally, it is not enough to be good, sincere, and loving. People who are good, wonderful, sincere, loving people—whether they are Mormon or wear the name Christian—won't go to heaven on that basis alone. It will be those who know Jesus Christ, and him crucified; who have surrendered their lives completely to him to serve him daily, enduring to the end.

Be radical for God!

Sheila Garrigus

I believe that the most important weapon we have is *prayer*. When more people are praying, there is more power. Whenever people come to me with the names of individuals in the Mormon church, the first thing I do is begin recruiting people to pray for them—not just for a day or a week; a commitment to pray for them as long as it takes.

I'm still praying for missionaries I met before I was ever baptized a Mormon. I'm still praying for dear friends in the church.

I'm expecting God to do something wonderful in their lives.

Granny Geer

I believe that Mormonism cannot be trusted. It began as a deliberate lie. Joseph Smith claimed what the Bible says is impossible and that he saw God. The Bible says, "No man has seen God at any time"(1 John 4:12). Mormonism is now led by liars who deliberately lie to promote and shield certain Mormon doctrines. Some Mormons are totally unaware that their leaders lie. For instance, Mormonism taught me to sing lies about the adoration of Joseph Smith (hymn: "Joseph the Seer") and a Heavenly Mother. Even when we sang true songs, like "The Old Rugged Cross," my Mormon leaders taught me to cling to Mormonism and Joseph Smith instead of to that cross, "stained with blood so divine."

For thirty-one years they taught me to sing "Rock of Ages," while teaching me to cling to the rock of Joseph Smith's purported revelations instead of to the Rock, Christ Jesus.

Praise God, I'm now free! I can sing the "new song" of salvation! But I want to be able to sing with my Mormon friends, "Round yon virgin, Mother and child," and explain to them how Mormonism has led them astray in the past and even today deliberately deceives their souls.

To that end I will continue to "pioneer for the real Jesus" as long as I am able to "go and tell." That's what Jesus bade me do forty-three years ago; and now, even though I'm "seventy-four going on seventeen," he is still saying, "Go and tell."

Kevin Bond

I believe that I came out of Mormonism in God's own perfect time, which gives me hope for my family and friends whom I love so dearly. They, too, are subject to God's timing.

I believe that while we who leave Mormonism need to make a clean break as far as doctrine goes, we must do it in a way that shows the change that Christ has made in us. Conviction, love, and peace will speak louder to the Mormons you leave behind than an attitude like a bull in a china shop who does irreparable damage while saying, "Get me out of here—get me out of here at all costs!"

Leaving Mormonism is incredibly difficult. It would have been much easier in some ways to just go back, to be reconciled with my parents, maintain my church status.

It was very hard to put away my patriarchal blessing, to acknowledge that it was not Scripture. It was a frightening experience to take off my temple garments for the last time and wonder—just in the back of my mind if all the stories about injury and death for those who did this were true.

Those were sobering experiences—but even more sobering than that was the death of my twin brother, Kris, in 1988. The heart defect that killed him was also detected in me, and I had surgery that kept me from suffering his fate. His death, therefore, wasn't for nothing; it saved my life.

I believe that my life has been spared so that I can tell the message of what it is like to have someone die so I can live. Two people—Kris and Christ—died, and I have been the direct beneficiary of both deaths. (Of course, the two deaths can't in another sense be compared fairly, for while one death merely postponed my physical death, the other has given me eternal life—quite a difference!)

Christians, like our Lord, have been anointed to preach to the poor, to proclaim freedom to the prisoner and sight to the blind, and to proclaim the year of the Lord's favor.

That, I know, is my new mission.

Sandra Tanner

First of all, there is a rock-bottom essential necessity when talking with Mormons: understanding their terminology. If a Christian isn't aware of the oddities of Mormon doctrine, he assumes that his Mormon friend is agreeing with him, and that they believe the same thing on major points.

Many Mormons themselves believe they are following the Bible. They are often ignorant of Mormon doctrine and just assume that it is found in the Bible. When I have shown Mormons what the Bible says on certain points, they have responded, "Yes, I believe that too." Then I can have a chance to tell them, "Well, I'm glad that you agree, for that is what the Bible teaches, but why would you want to stay in a church where your leaders don't believe that? If these men are prophets, seers, and revelators, why do they teach doctrine that is different from what you and I have just agreed that the Bible teaches?"

A Christian who wants to witness to a Mormon should also have a good overall view of the Mormon doctrine of eternal progression. Not only will this help in discussion with a Mormon, but once a Christian realizes the depths of deception that the Mormon has endured, a Christian will have a greater burden for the Mormon.

Once a Mormon realizes himself the profundity of this deception, they will often feel emotions of anger and bitterness.

Some of these are valid, at least temporarily—who wouldn't feel betrayed by being told lies that affect your soul's salvation? But these negative emotions must be replaced by what Ephesians 4:29–32 teaches: kindness, gentleness, forgiveness—even forgiveness of the church leaders who knowingly taught these lies.

Even though Jerald and I have spent the last thirty years of our lives opposing Mormonism and its doctrine, I can honestly say that I do not feel anger or bitterness toward Mormons. Over the years I realized that I don't have to win every argument or have the last word in every conversation. I can give a word for Christ, and if it is rejected, I can move on and leave it up to the Holy Spirit to use what has been said.

Latayne Scott

I would like to make two points about Mormonism, and both of them have to do with motivations.

The first thing I would say is to Christians, and would answer the question that so many people ask me: "Why would anyone want to *become* a Mormon?"

In general people become Mormons for the same reason that people become Christians: they believe that what they are doing is pleasing to God, and will enable them to serve him better. To assign devious motives to the sincere believers in Mormon doctrine is both arrogant and blind, and will ultimately damage your own effectiveness in reaching those Mormons.

The other statement I would make to Mormons who want to know (most of them sincerely) why I, and the others in this book are "attacking" their church. (Mormon readers of this book will doubtless ask this very question.)

In response to this, I refer my Mormon friends to the *Pearl of Great Price*, Joseph Smith chapter 2, verse 19. There Joseph Smith said that when he was asked which church he was to join, he was told by "God" to join none of them, for "all their creeds were an abomination in his sight, that those professors were all corrupt; that: 'they draw near to me with their lips, but their hearts are far from me. . . .'"

This is what Joseph Smith, almost 150 years ago, taught all Mormons to believe about Christians.

So who fired the first shot in this battle? Are not we Christians the ones who must historically defend ourselves against what Mormonism teaches about us?

Epilogue

It has to be obvious, after reading the accounts of these eight very different people, that there is after all no one secret password of information you can give to your Mormon friends that will cause them to see the false nature of Mormonism. That is because each friend is certainly not exactly like any of the people in this book, who in turn are very dissimilar to each other. Only by listening to each can we see similarities to the people we know, and thus take our cue on those things that would be meaningful to our friends.

Those who have left Mormonism are often asked for a certain "technique" to be used to help convert a friend or loved one out of Mormonism, and I have found that often this is not so much a request for information as rather a plea for help in knowing how hard to "push." While I do not know the answer for this in each situation, I can say that I have learned something interesting about how ex-Mormons respond to such a query. After talking to and corresponding with ex-Mormons for ten years, and now after interviewing the seven people in this book, I have noticed that the longer people are away from Mormonism, the more inclined they are to be assertive—even aggressive—in dealing with Mormons. Take, for instance, the no-holds-barred approach of long-time believer Granny Geer who "goes for the jugular," immediately confronting a Mormon with the shockingly sexual implications of his theology before she knows his first name. Contrast that with the repeated cautions of, say, Kevin Bond whose exodus from Mormonism is much more recent and who insists on gentleness in witnessing to Mormons. I know this generalization does not hold true in all cases, nonetheless I believe that it is true in my own experience and that of many others: that the longer you are away from Mormonism, the more bold—or even brassy—you become in confronting its errors.

Writing this book brought me to other new conclusions too. Sometimes they were just rediscoveries of facts I already knew. For instance, I have always assumed that each person is important to God, no matter what his or her earthly status. But why was I amazed that the struggles of a young woman picking cotton in Arizona would impact the thousands of souls that Granny Geer has? Why should a disagreement in a church service on a remote Pacific island really matter in anyone else's life except that of the listening Dave Wilkins? Why would a no-show guest speaker at a Christian businessmen's meeting make a difference to anyone but Sheila Garrigus? The thought that God was there in each of these circumstances, working his perfect will in human lives through very ordinary circumstances, has sobered me: if these people are that important to God, I have concluded, then they should be important to me—they, and others like them.

I say that because I have seen an attitude in Christians I know who seem to "grade" people as prospective Christians. Somehow or other we have gotten the idea that we get "extra points" for helping in the conversion process of certain people. In teaching Mormons this means that it is somehow "better" or more meritorious to convert a bishop descended from Brigham Young than, say, someone who was converted to Mormonism as an adult, or who has become inactive. But God, I think, sees them all as equals in value—and so should we.

I say that as a note of caution as much to myself as to anyone else. It would only be our own human point of view that would say, for instance, that gung-ho Mormon Cindy Bauer was a better "catch" for the kingdom than a coffee-drinking Dave Wilkins who had drifted away from Mormonism years before making a decision for Christ. As the parable of the great net in Matthew 13:47–49 teaches us, the kingdom of heaven pulls in all kinds, and we have not the angelic discernment to grade its fishes.

Nor can we say that those who have been very public in telling the world of their conversion experiences are more highly esteemed in God's eyes than less vocal people. I purposely chose a mixture of well-known and little-known ex-Mormons for this book. One reason for this is that thousands of Mormons will leave their church and become faithful, productive Christians without ever writing a book or addressing a crowd about why they left. Not everyone can write; not everyone can speak in public. But this I know: at the end of time, those faithful ex-Mormon Christians who shone their lights and used their spiritual gifts in their own circles will be just as loved, just as welcome in heaven, as any book writer or public speaker among us.

This thought reminds me of one of my favorite stories, that of a young man who was walking along a seashore. Ahead of him, he saw in the distance an old man walking who every few steps would stoop down to pick something up and throw it into the sea. As the young man came closer, he saw that the old man was picking up starfish which had been beached by the tide. There were hundreds of these starfish, and the young man hurried with irritation to catch up with the old man.

"Why are you bothering to pick up these starfish?" he asked. "There are so many, you can't possibly save them all. What does it matter?"

The old man stooped and picked up yet another starfish, flinging it into the waves. "It mattered to this one," he said.

And as I look into the eyes of a child like Matthew Bond

or Jamie Garrigus or Lori Wilkins, I too can say, "It mattered to this one."

There are other conclusions which compiling this book brought me to as well. One is the reaffirmation of the truth that Paul wrote of when he described the conversion process as one in which someone can plant a seed, another will water it, but it is God himself who gives the increase, and that in his own good time.

Sandra Tanner once commented that this process is many faceted, often an exposure of the mind to different points of view and different people. Often this exposure causes a person to push unsettling new information to the back of his or her mind, where it will often stay undisturbed for months or years. When finally a document or Scripture "clicks" in the mind, that alone is usually not solely responsible for forcing a change of thinking; it is the accumulation of many "stored away" items of information—like the pamphlet on Granny Geer's cabinet or the tract in Cindy Bauer's pocket—that combines with something else. And that, it seems, forces a point of departure.

Looking back, it seems that many of the people in this book would say that what first caused them to doubt Mormonism were not maneuvered strategies, planned by someone else, to cause them to doubt. As in the case of Dave Wilkins who instinctively knew that Christians should be known by their love for each other and was repelled by the fighting he saw in a church meeting, it is often the response of an individual's conscience that is the first clue that something is wrong. Some people would say that this is the action of the Holy Spirit on a receptive mind; others would explain that it is the yearning for the Shepherd's voice that his sheep have, rejecting all substitutes. One thing is certain: God will convey his messages to those he has chosen, and we who are sometimes the conduits of his Word can rein in our too-proud hearts with the knowledge that he, who can make donkeys and rocks talk if he so pleases, speaks often most clearly in his own still, small voice.

Once that voice—in whatever form—is heard and has an effect on the heart of a Mormon, those of us who stand observing that process are often frustrated with the pace we see. Even once a Mormon has renounced his old faith and embraced the truth, sometimes he will hold onto vestigial elements of Mormonism. An example: much to the annoyance of some Christians, Jerald and Sandra Tanner were still believers in the *Book of Mormon* two years after they had turned from the Utah-based Latter-day Saint group's other doctrines and had accepted Christ.

I have often compared the mind's grasp of theological tenets as being like a bucket filled with information. When one leaves Mormonism and becomes a Christian, you cannot "dump out" everything you've ever learned about religion—the Bible, revelation, human ethics, and so forth—and start fresh with an empty bucket. Instead, you must reach into that bucket and examine each item piece by piece, replacing those which are faulty with new information. (That is why I, as a year-old Christian, could talk blithely about Colossians 1:15 which states that Jesus is made in the image of the invisible God, saying to a horrified Sunday school class that this meant Jesus' body and God's looked alike.)

This replacement of erroneous information with truth is common to any change of religious thinking: for instance, one does not make the choice to leave the Presbyterian church and become a Quaker without replacing doctrinal or practical ideas. The transition from Mormonism to Christianity, however, has some elements that are unique. One involves the element of the demonic, such as was mentioned by Sheila Garrigus. Now I have met and talked with Sheila, eaten in her home, and had her in my own. She is neither wild-eyed nor irrational. She concluded that the image of her grandmother which she saw telling her to remain faithful in the Mormon church was a demonic deception. But even if this had some other explanation, we are left with the effect that this must have had on Sheila and others like her—an effect that lasted until even after leaving Mormonism. Can you imagine the fear involved in going to your knees before God, asking for guidance and knowing that the last time you did so, you received clear instruction that was ungodly?

It is because of precisely such things that people who are leaving Mormonism have two acute needs: solid Bible teaching and warm (even sacrificial) fellowship. These are both essentials, nonnegotiable and irreplaceable. Without the first, the new ex-Mormon Christians will go from one system of error to another; without the second they will wither and die no matter how biblical the teaching they receive. That is why those who participated in this book remember with special fondness the meals and conversation on which their hungry souls fed after leaving a church that in most cases had been not only a way of thinking but a way of life.

People who leave Mormonism have another type of problem that is not common to those who leave other religions. I am sure it has not escaped the attention of anyone who read the accounts in this book that often Mormon church leaders advised Mormons to leave their non-Mormon or ex-Mormon spouses. This specter of divorce is a powerful weapon in spiritual warfare, one that is used equally effectively as threat and as punishment. We Christians who counsel a Mormon to leave his or her church must realize that their choice to leave behind its doctrines is sometimes like a contract that includes an unwelcome "rider," one over which they have no control once they decide to follow Jesus. At such a time we must offer them more than a be-ye-warmed-and-filled pat on the back and a glib quoting of Luke 18:29. There is no hurt like the hurt of loneliness.

The cost of leaving Mormonism is for many people almost impossibly high. I know I speak for the other participants in this book when I say that while none of us want to be thought of as martyrs, we must make the Christian community aware of the price they are asking their Mormon friends to pay to leave behind the very real elements of comfort and solidity in Mormonism in exchange for benefits we must honestly tell them are guaranteed only in heaven.

New Christians who come out of Mormonism are not just "new-born babes," they are newborns that are born addicted. They come to the Christian body with special needs that must be met or they will die. They must be weaned away from extrabiblical "scriptures" and empty promises of a celestial kingdom and godhood. They need extra warmth, extra love to help them through inevitable and devastating withdrawal.

Leaving Mormonism involves more than being willing to give up a way of life or family. It means giving up your god. In making a transition from one mainstream denomination to another, you might be called upon to change the way you worship, or make certain lifestyle adjustments. In more dramatic "relocations" within Christianity, one might even have to reassess how one views the God he or she worships, as with the discovery that the stern God of your childhood is really One of mercy and grace; or that the lax, all-inclusive Deity you once perceived has on closer examination shown himself to be One who requires absolute loyalty to himself.

Only in the case of someone who comes out of a pagan religion (Hinduism, for instance) or one who leaves a "Christian cult" such as Mormonism is a more complete change made. We who have left Mormonism have found that the (theoretically) tangible, flesh-and-bones, anthropomorphic, formerly human god we worshiped was a myth. We have replaced him with a God who is spirit (at least in this life), unseeable, untouchable, and very much unlike us except as we strive to be like him.

For all this, though, he is certainly more approachable than the tactile god of Mormonism, for he, after all, does exist.

May that inescapable reality continue to guide us all.

Glossary

The following is a listing of informal definitions of terms used in this book that may be unfamiliar to non-Mormon readers.

Adam-God doctrine—early teachings by Brigham Young and others that identified Adam as being God.

Bear one's testimony—to state aloud one's beliefs, especially that the LDS church is the only true church.

Bishop—head of a ward.

Bishop's court—ecclesiastical setting in which an excommunication or other disciplinary action is pronounced.

Burning in the bosom—physical reaction promised by the *Book of Mormon* to all who ask God to verify the truthfulness of the *Book of Mormon*.

Celestial Kingdom—highest level of heaven.

Chapel—meetinghouse of an LDS ward.

Communion—weekly observance of the Lord's Supper, consisting of bread and water.

Confirmation—brief ceremony following baptism in which a new member is told to receive the Holy Spirit.

Doctrine and Covenants—scripture of the LDS church that records early "revelations" and official proclamations.

Elder—lowest office of the Melchizedek, or higher, priesthood.

Endowments—secret ceremony containing oaths, handshakes, and instructions; takes place only in a temple.

Eternal progression—LDS doctrine that claims that all humans and gods are constantly advancing in quality or "goodness."

Exaltation—*see* Salvation by grace alone.

Fast offering—contribution given once a month which equals the value of meals which are missed for spiritual reasons.

General Authority—high official of the LDS church.

Gentile—any non-Mormon (even a Jew).

Institute of Religion—on-campus theological center for college students.

Investigator—non-Mormon who is studying Mormon doctrine.

"Jack Mormon"—LDS member who is either inactive or who does not live the Mormon lifestyle.

Journal of Discourses—multi-volume set of transcripts of early LDS sermons.

Ministering angel—the status of servanthood in the Celestial Kingdom; the fate of all faithful Mormons who were not married in a temple.

Moroni—character in the *Book of Mormon.*

Mutual Improvement Association (MIA)—youth organization of the LDS Church.

Nephites—ancient people supposed to have lived in the Americas as recorded in the *Book of Mormon.*

Patriarchal blessing—official, recorded pronouncement of a LDS official (usually elderly) which tells the listener which tribe of Israel he or she belongs to, as well as predictions about his or her future life.

Pearl of Great Price—book of Mormon scripture which purports to include writings of Moses, Abraham, and Joseph Smith.

Preexistence—state in which all people existed before being born on earth.

Priesthood—"the authority to act for God"; contains two branches: Aaronic (lesser) and Melchizedek (greater).

Primary—children's organization of the LDS church.

Relief Society—women's auxiliary of the LDS church.

Reorganized Church of Jesus Christ of Latter Day Saints—largest "splinter group" of Mormonism, centered in Independence, MO; believes in the *Book of Mormon* but not in later LDS scriptures.

Returned missionary—"R.M."— someone who has completed a mission for the LDS church.

Sacrament meeting—Sunday meeting, attendance at which is mandatory for good standing in church.

Salvation by grace alone—equated with universal resurrection. **Exaltation**, or eternal life, refers to where one spends eternity. Salvation is free, but exaltation must be earned.

Seminary—weekday classes for high-school age youth.

Seventy—missionary-developing branch of the LDS priesthood.

Stake—a group of wards; headed by a stake president.

Temple—special worship site closed to all but the most faithful Mormons; where vicarious and in-person endowments, sealings, and baptisms take place.

Temple recommend—certificate that allows a Mormon to enter a temple, obtained after a stringent interview with a bishop.

Tracting—going from door-to-door, setting up appointments for missionary lessons or "discussions."

Ward—a congregation of Mormons, defined usually by geographical boundaries and presided over by a bishop.

Word of Wisdom—health law that forbids use of hot drinks (defined as coffee and tea), tobacco, alcoholic beverages.

Reading List of Materials Written by Participants

Thelma "Granny" Geer:

Mormonism, Mama, and Me! (Moody, 1986)

Sandra Tanner:

The Bible and Mormon Doctrine

(with Jerald Tanner):

Mormonism: Shadow or Reality? (Modern Microfilm, 1972)
The Changing World of Mormonism (Moody, 1980)
Major Problems of Mormonism (Utah Lighthouse Ministry, 1989)
Mormon Scriptures and the Bible
A Look at Christianity
Mormonism, Magic, and Masonry
Joseph Smith and Moneydigging
Archaeology and the Book of Mormon
Tracking the White Salamander
Did Spaulding Write the Book of Mormon?
Can the Browns Save Joseph Smith?
Mormonism, Hughes, and the CIA
Unmasking a Mormon Spy

The Tanners on Trial
Joseph Smith and Polygamy
Mormonism Like Watergate?
Mormonism and Negroes
The Mormon Kingdom, Volumes 1 and 2
The Case Against Mormonism, Volumes 1, 2, 3
Changes in Joseph Smith's History
Falsification of Joseph Smith's History
A Critical Look—A Study of the Overstreet "Confession"
Answering Dr. Clandestine
Changes in the Key to Theology

Books by Latayne Scott:

The Mormon Mirage (Zondervan, 1979, 1988)

Open Up Your Life: A Woman's Workshop on Hospitality (Zondervan, 1983)

To Love Each Other: A Woman's Workshop on 1 Corinthians 13 (Zondervan, 1985)

Time, Talents, Things: A Woman's Workshop on Christian Stewardship (Zondervan, 1987)

Crisis: Crucible of Praise (Zondervan, 1989)

A Marriage Made in Heaven: The Eternal Love of the Bride and Bridegroom (Word, 1990)